THE
FIFTY MIRACLE PRINCIPLES
OF
A COURSE IN MIRACLES

Third Edition

Kenneth Wapnick, Ph.D.

Foundation for "A Course in Miracles"

Foundation for "A Course in Miracles"
R.R. 2, Box 71
Roscoe, NY 12776-9506

First edition, 1985
Second printing, 1987
Second edition, 1990
Third edition, 1992

Printed in the United States of America

Library of Congress Cataloging in Publication Data

Wapnick, Kenneth
    The fifty miracle principles of a Course in miracles / Kenneth Wapnick.
    -- 3rd ed.
        p.   cm.
    Combined transcripts of two one-day workshops held Jan. 6 and Jan. 13, 1985.
    ISBN 0-933291-15-9
    1. Course in miracles. 2. Spiritual life. I. Title.
BP605.C68W3587 1992
299'.93--dc20   92-28257
                                                                      CIP

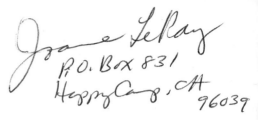

The Fifty Miracle Principles of
A COURSE IN MIRACLES

PREFACE TO THE THIRD EDITION

For this new edition, the book has again been retypeset. However, virtually no changes have been made from the second edition, except in the notation for references to *A Course in Miracles*. This was necessitated by the recently published (1992) second edition of the Course, which was retypeset and contains numbering for all paragraphs and sentences, as well as for the chapters and sections of the text, lessons and introductions in the workbook for students, questions in the manual for teachers, and the terms in the clarification of terms. Thus, references to *A Course in Miracles* are now given in two ways: the first, unchanged from before, cites the pages found in the first edition; the second is now consistent with the numbering system of the second edition. An example from each book follows:

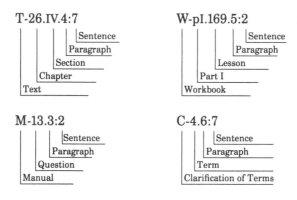

PREFACE TO THE SECOND EDITION

This revised edition has been entirely retypeset. However, aside from some minor stylistic revisions, and inclusion of specific Course references to quotations and allusions, the material and its informal style has been unchanged. I am grateful to Rosemarie LoSasso, the Foundation's Publications Director, for her, as always, careful and caring supervision of this printing.

PREFACE TO THE FIRST EDITION

This is a combined transcript of two one-day workshops on the Fifty Miracle Principles, which were the first workshops I gave at our Teaching and Healing Center.* These workshops— on January 6 and 13, 1985—basically consisted of the same subject matter. The basis for this pamphlet was the workshop of January 13, supplemented by material from the first workshop that was not repeated in the second. Some additional material was added to clarify certain points, as well as minor revisions made to improve readability. As is explained during the workshop, the basic format involved my analyzing the Fifty Miracle Principles line by line. This procedure was interspersed with questions from the group, which allowed for further discussion of the principles and related ideas.

The tapes of the workshop on January 6 are available in a three ninety-minute cassette album for $24.00, and may be ordered from the Foundation for "A Course in Miracles," R.R. 2, Box 71, Roscoe, NY 12776.

I am very grateful to my wife, Gloria, who prepared the initial editing of the manuscript by reviewing and correcting the transcript of the second workshop, comparing it to the tapes of the first one. This greatly facilitated the final editing of this pamphlet.

---

*In 1988, the Foundation was relocated from Crompond, NY, to Roscoe, NY, and the name of the Center was changed to the Conference and Retreat Center.

INTRODUCTION

The workshop began with a meditation, with Gloria reading "What is a Miracle?":

A miracle is a correction. It does not create, nor really change at all. It merely looks on devastation, and reminds the mind that what it sees is false. It undoes error, but does not attempt to go beyond perception, nor exceed the function of forgiveness. Thus it stays within time's limits. Yet it paves the way for the return of timelessness and love's awakening, for fear must slip away under the gentle remedy it brings.

A miracle contains the gift of grace, for it is given and received as one. And thus it illustrates the law of truth the world does not obey, because it fails entirely to understand its ways. A miracle inverts perception which was upside down before, and thus it ends the strange distortions that were manifest. Now is perception open to the truth. Now is forgiveness seen as justified.

Forgiveness is the home of miracles. The eyes of Christ deliver them to all they look upon in mercy and in love. Perception stands corrected in His sight, and what was meant to curse has come to bless. Each lily of forgiveness offers all the world the silent miracle of love. And each is laid before the Word of God, upon the universal altar to Creator and creation in the light of perfect purity and endless joy.

The miracle is taken first on faith, because to ask for it implies the mind has been made ready to conceive of what it cannot see and does not understand. Yet faith will bring its witnesses to show that what it rested on is really there. And thus the miracle will justify your faith in it, and show it rested on a world more real than what you saw before; a world redeemed from what you thought was there.

Miracles fall like drops of healing rain from Heaven on a dry and dusty world, where starved and thirsty creatures come to die. Now they have water. Now the world is green. And everywhere the signs of life spring up, to show that what is born can never die, for what has life has immortality.

(workbook, p. 463; W-pII.13)

A month or two ago when Gloria and I were first talking about what we should do in this workshop, Gloria suggested the idea of our doing these miracle principles. This is not my

1

favorite part in the text, but then I was reminded of the statement in *Alice in Wonderland* where the King says that you begin at the beginning, then you go until the end, and then you stop. Since this is the way *A Course in Miracles* begins, it seems like a logical place for us to begin, too.

What we will do after I make some introductory comments is go through these fifty principles line by line. You will see that this first section starts almost like an operatic overture, in that it contains most of the major themes that are found fully developed later in the text; and, like many operatic overtures, I do not think it is as good as the actual opera or book.

I thought I would spend the first part of this workshop explaining how I see these fifty principles and also trying to account for what seem to be inconsistencies in some of them as they are compared to statements found later on in the text. I think people who read this opening section carefully, as well as the first four or five chapters, would find that there are certain things there that do not quite seem to fit with what comes later. And, certainly, the style of the writing is not on the same level. There are reasons for this which I would like to share.

Most of you, I am sure, are familiar with the story of how *A Course in Miracles* came to be written. Helen Schucman, a psychologist, heard Jesus' voice speak to her, and he dictated these three volumes. When the process first began in October of 1965, for the first four weeks or so, Helen found herself in a very anxiety-producing situation. While this did not interfere with the basic content of what she heard, it certainly did interfere, I think, with the clarity with which she heard.

Helen had intimations that she had long ago developed this scribal ability, misused it, and left it dormant for quite some time. If you have a faucet that has not been used for some time, and you suddenly turn on the water, you would have a lot of rust. The water comes through, but at the beginning you have a lot of discoloration. I think that is what you find here: the material itself is consistent with the basic teaching of the Course, but the mode of expression is not consistent.

Very often Helen would write down something and the following day Jesus would say to her, in effect, "This is what you wrote down yesterday; this is what it should be," and would correct a lot of the stylistic inconsistencies as well as some of the awkwardness of the language. So I think it is even more important to understand how these early chapters were written. Beginning with Chapter 5, you can almost feel the text moving into a higher gear in terms of its language and clarity of expression. The important point is that right at the beginning, it was not really straight dictation. It was as if Jesus were having an ongoing conversation with Helen, where he would say things and Helen would ask him questions or he would anticipate questions in her mind. A lot of the earlier conversations had to do with helping Helen and Bill integrate this material with their own professional backgrounds as well as their personal lives.

As all of us know, we talk one way when we are having an informal conversation, and express ourselves quite another way when we write things down. I know from my own experience, when I talk to people informally or in my office I will talk one way, and not pay too much attention to what I am saying— whether the words are consistent with other things I have said. When I am writing a book or an article, it is much different. Then I am much more careful. I think that this is exactly the situation that occurred in those early weeks, as can be seen especially in the first four chapters. This explains, I think, why there are certain inconsistencies in how the text expresses itself in the beginning chapters, and why much of the writing seems awkward and surely not on the same high literary level as the rest of the material. Certainly, also, a lot of the personal material which Helen had written down was not meant for the general public and had to be taken out. It was really meant only for her and for Bill. So, again, this would explain why there is a certain awkwardness in the writing.

Let me mention one of the inconsistencies you will find, which is basically what we will be talking about today: what a miracle is, the subject of *A Course in Miracles*. One of the principles which we will be covering later speaks of a miracle as healing. In Chapter 2, Jesus says, "To speak of 'a miracle of healing' is to combine two orders of reality inappropriately" (text, p. 19; T-2.IV.1:3). Yet, near the end of the text there are a few references which talk about a "miracle of healing" (e.g., text, p. 529; T-27.II.5:2). This apparent inconsistency is explained by keeping in mind the circumstances of the writing. In some of the early miracle principles, "miracle" is used almost in the way we would popularly use it: to talk about an external act, where there is some external shift in the world or someone's behavior. As becomes very clear in some of the other principles, and certainly is the central theme of the Course, a miracle is a correction in perception, just as in the workbook passage Gloria read; it is a correction in how we perceive and how we think. But there are, certainly, principles that seem to imply a change in behavior. In Chapter 2, when Jesus specifically talks about what healing is and begins a series of sections on that (text, p. 19; T-2.IV), he is making a distinction between the miracle which is the shift in thought, and then the effect which would be healing. Later on in the book when those earlier explanations and distinctions are no longer necessary, the Course is much more poetic and, therefore, could be called somewhat loose in its expression and would then use the phrase "a miracle of healing."

There is another miracle principle (21) that talks about God's forgiveness, while in the workbook there is a very clear statement, in fact it is repeated, which says that "God does not forgive because He has never condemned" (workbook, pp. 73, 99; W-pI.46.1:1; W-pI.60.1:2). Forgiveness is a correction for a hostile or angry thought. And since obviously God does not have those thoughts, there is no need for correction or forgiveness in Heaven. In the popular use of the word, however, we do speak of the forgiveness of God. In fact, one of the lovelier passages in the text, which is the Course's version of the Lord's Prayer, begins with the words, "Forgive us our illusions, Father" (text, p. 326; T-16.VII.12:1). So if you are looking for inconsistencies in the Course, you are going to find them. If you want to make trouble with Jesus, and use the various inconsistencies as a way of disproving or taking issue with his Course, then you do not have to go past page one or two. In fact, in the early months, Helen was trying very hard to do that, and he told her he wished she would not do that because it was wasting a lot of time.

4

Overall, one of the most remarkable things about *A Course in Miracles* is its consistency from beginning to end in what it teaches and what it says. It never deviates from that; but its expressions are not always quite as consistent. Before we actually start going through the fifty principles line by line, I would like to put something on the board as a way of orienting us in our discussion of miracles. None of us was very happy with the title that Jesus gave to the Course, but he seemed clear that he wanted to call it *A Course in Miracles*. So, it is the miracle that is the primary concern, and that is what we are really being taught. The miracle, once again, has nothing to do with anything external, the major reason being that there is nothing external.

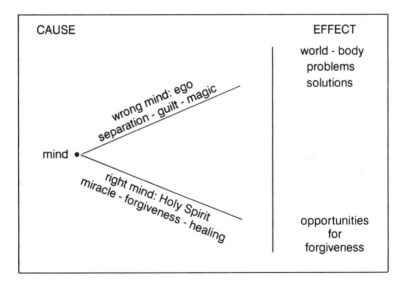

Today we are not going to go into the Course's metaphysics; we are going to assume that we accept that principle. But, certainly, the basic metaphysical foundation of the Course is that there is no world outside us. It is only a projection of what is inside us, which means that the central issue always can be found in the little dot over there on the left side of the chart, which represents the mind. The mind projects what is within it onto the world; and the world, of course, includes not only the world at large, the universe, but also the world of our personal bodies. This means that the problem is never what is outside us here in the world. The problem is always what is in our minds; and since that is where the problem is, that is where the answer must be found also. That answer is the miracle.

The best definition of what a miracle is, then, is that it is a correction for a misthinking or a misperception, and therefore *A Course in Miracles* will never advocate that you do anything about changing your behavior. Many of you may have seen the article on the Course in the *New York Times* about a month ago (Dec. 9, 1984) in which I was quoted backwards. The quote said that you should change your behavior, and that changes your mind. I am sure I said the exact opposite to them on the phone: that your change of mind will correspondingly shift your behavior. This does not mean, by the way, that the Course would not advocate many times doing something to shift your behavior. All that it would say is that you not believe that by changing your behavior you have changed the problem. It could be a useful step towards changing a problem, but the basic problem is never out in the world or the body—it is in the mind. This idea, of course, is absolutely essential to everything that the Course teaches and everything that we will be talking about. Certainly it is essential for understanding what the miracle is. The simplest definition of a miracle is that it is a correction for how we perceive or for how we think.

One of my favorite lines in the Course, which really is a perfect definition of a miracle even though it does not use the word, says that "the holiest of all the spots on earth is where an ancient hatred has become a present love" (text, p. 522; T-26. IX.6:1). Someone whom we hate, hatred being the ego's way of looking becomes someone whom we love, and that vision of love is given to us by the Holy Spirit. What we are talking about are two different ways of looking at the world and, more specifically, looking at the relationships in our lives. One is the ego's way of looking, which is a way of seeing more and more separation, anger and guilt, justifying our anger, and making sickness real here in the body. All these perceptions really reinforce the basic ego premise that we are separate from each other and from God. The correction for that is to go from the ego's way of looking to the Holy Spirit's way of looking, and it is that shift from the ego to the Holy Spirit that is the miracle. The identical word for that process of shifting from the ego's perceptions of someone else to the Holy Spirit's, is "forgiveness."

When we do forgive, what we are really doing is healing the problem, because the basic source of the problem is our interpretation of it, and this is based on our guilt. So all of our problems—whether they be physical, financial, or social—are not found out here in the world of the body but are found, rather, in our minds, and they all can be traced back to a problem of guilt. Another term for guilt would be "lack of forgiveness." It is when we forgive that our problems are healed, so we can then say that the words "miracle," "forgiveness," and "healing" represent basically the same process.

We can see, therefore, that a miracle is the answer to the problem, which is guilt, and we can define this even further and say that all of guilt comes from the belief that we are separate. So, these two words, "separation" and "guilt," are also virtually synonymous, because one comes from the other.

Are there any questions at this point, before we actually start with the principles?

Q: When you speak of forgiveness, are you speaking of forgiveness of self, and then others?

A: The basic Course process is that we forgive ourselves through forgiving others, so that, technically, you forgive someone else and that, correspondingly, enables you to forgive yourself. In our experience it is a reciprocal process. The more that I forgive you, the more forgiven I will feel. The more forgiven I feel, the easier it is for me to forgive other people. But, in terms of the basic paradigm *A Course in Miracles* sets forth, we forgive someone else, and then, correspondingly, we forgive ourselves because it is the same thing. Once we accept the idea that there is nothing out there in the world except what we put there, we recognize a direct link between what is in our minds and what we see. If you recall, the early workbook lessons are very clear in training us to think that way, and they make it very clear that there is no distinction between what we perceive outside and what we perceive inside—that it is our thoughts that make up the world. So we are really talking about one and the same thing.

The importance of recognizing the primacy of forgiving someone out there is that most of this guilt in our minds is unconscious—we are not aware of it. This means that if we do not see a problem, we cannot do anything about it. But usually we can become aware of the negative feelings we feel towards other people, so that if I find myself getting annoyed with you out here, and I am looking at you properly, I am letting the Holy Spirit guide me in how I am perceiving and understanding what is happening. Then He will tell me that whatever it is I am holding against you is really the mirror of what I am holding against myself, except that I did not know that I was holding it against myself. This is because, again, most guilt is unconscious. By your coming into my life and being such a problem for me, you are enabling me, by virtue of your being a mirror, to look at you and see reflected back exactly what is inside myself. By changing my mind about something I have accused you of, what I am really doing is changing my mind about something I have accused myself of. However, the form can be different. So what we are really talking about is the very important term which does not appear in this first section at all, and that term is "projection": we project what is in our minds onto the world.

Q: Would you say, in order to be open to this and to understand it that you would really have to be asking the Holy Spirit for help all the time?

A: Yes, *A Course in Miracles* makes it very clear that it is impossible to truly forgive someone without the Holy Spirit's help because our egos are so strongly entrenched in our minds. This is really saying that our investment in maintaining the illusion of separation and of guilt is so entrenched in our minds, that it is almost impossible, if not completely impossible, to actually change our minds without outside help. That outside help, the Holy Spirit of course, is really inside. As the Course frequently quotes from the gospels: Of ourselves we can do nothing (e.g., manual, p. 67; M-29.4:2).

Q: In talking to my friend here, I found that I was projecting something onto her, then I found that there was an inner projection within myself, but I found that it was not within myself in relation to her, it was within myself in relation to God, an entirely different subject, but the same projection.

A: The bottom line, always, is our relationship with God. The bottom line in the ego system of anyone is the belief that we are separate from God, that we have attacked God, and God is angry at us and is going to punish us. That constellation of thoughts is central to everyone's ego, and in order to escape from the wrath of God, we endure all kinds of peculiar things, the most peculiar of which is the belief that by attacking someone else—in other words, projecting the problem from ourselves onto someone else—we could be free of the problem. So that the interpersonal problems we experience, when you really examine them, all have to do with somehow believing that the other person is separate from us. From that, then, follows the belief that this other person has victimized us, or we turn around and feel guilty because we believe we have victimized them.

Those experiences we can all identify with. We all have lots of different opportunities in our lives to recognize how that works. But all of them come back to the basic problem which is that we believe we are separated from God, which in turn means we believe we have attacked Him, and this means we believe we have victimized Him, that He is the victim of us. Then we turn that around, because projection always follows from guilt, and we believe that God is victimizing us. So within the ego system, death, for example, becomes the most glaring witness to the reality of God's wrath. God created a body, which on one level is what the ego believes, and then He punishes the body by destroying it—He makes the body suffer, etc.

That, again, is the rock bottom line in everyone's unconscious, and then all we do is project that over and over again onto everyone else. As the Course teaches, you cannot get right back to Heaven because the amount of fear and terror that is contained here is awesome. What we can do is begin nibbling away at that thought system, and we begin the nibbling with all the people with whom we are currently in a relationship. And we can be in a relationship with people whether we are physically with them or we just think of them. So, someone who died twenty or thirty years ago may still be very present in our minds because we are still carrying around past hurts, or past illusions about that person.

Anything else? Okay, let us start, then, by talking about the fifty principles.

Principle 1

There is no order of difficulty in miracles. One is not "harder" or "bigger" than another. They are all the same. All expressions of love are maximal.

While I said that this is not my favorite section, I think that the first principle, really, is a gem. It is one of the most important statements in the whole book, and I think Jesus thinks so too, because it is a principle that occurs over and over again in all three books in many different forms. If we could thoroughly understand what it means, that "there is no order of difficulty in miracles," we would understand everything else in the Course, because that principle contains within it the seed of the entire thought system. That "there is no order of difficulty in miracles" is the same thing as saying that all the problems in the world are really the same—the seemingly major ones and the seemingly minor ones. There is no difference among them.

This can be thoroughly understood only when you recognize that there is no world out there. If you believe in the reality of the perceptual, physical, or separated world, then you must believe that there are gradations: there are bigger things and there are smaller things. Our entire world, which really is to say the entire world of perception, is based upon orders and differences. We all have concepts of large and small, fat and thin, beautiful and ugly, male and female, night and day, light and darkness, large problems, small problems, and on and on and on. Our idea of colors is also based on that: different wave lengths of light. These are all inherent parts of the ego's world of separation—that there are differences in this world.

Once we believe that the body is real, we will then believe that there are certain problems that are more critical than others. If a person has a sickness that is "life threatening," then that is a serious problem. If a person has a mild headache, then we say that that is not such a serious problem. There is no one in this world who does not fall into that trap. It also takes the form of asking the Holy Spirit's help for some problems and not others; or believing that He is too busy to bother with our inconsequential and silly problems; or believing that we can take care of this by ourselves. In truth, however, we are afraid of His solution, for that would mean the undoing of the ego.

However, the purpose of studying *A Course in Miracles* is not to have us feel guilty because we fall into these traps. The whole idea of the Course is to let us know just how insane we are and how insane this thought system is, so we could change our minds about it. You cannot change your mind about something if you do not know it is there. So, the idea of exposing the ego's thought system is not to make us feel even more guilty than we do, or more stupid than we may feel, but to help us realize that, in fact, we do believe this, so we then can change our minds about it. And this first principle really starts us off with a bang.

What this means, then, is that it is just as easy to heal a cancer as it is to heal a mild headache. It is just as easy to heal a threat of nuclear war as it is to heal an argument between two little kids, because they are all the same thing. They all stem from one center point, which is the belief in separation or the belief in guilt. The problems are never out there in the world, but within our minds. The things that we do in this world to alleviate pain are all done on the symptom level, which means they are all done on the level of form. One of the key principles in the Course is the distinction that we are always asked to make between form and content. *A Course in Miracles* teaches that there are only two basic contents in the world: God or the ego; love or fear; spirit or the body. There are only two basic perceptions in the world: one is the ego's way of looking at a problem, the other is the Holy Spirit's way of looking at a problem.

What happens is that these contents then come in a myriad number of forms. When we say that the basic content in the ego's world is separation, then it is obvious to us just how many different forms this belief takes. Some things we call negative, like pain, suffering, death, etc. Some we call positive, which usually means that we get what we want, or that people are free from external suffering. But the issue is never the form, which is on the right side of the chart; the issue is always the underlying thought, on the left (see p. 5).

In Chapter 23 there is a section called "The Laws of Chaos" (text, p. 455; T-23.II) which is a very difficult section and one of the most important ones in the text. "The Laws of Chaos" describes the five laws that comprise the ego's thought system, which actually are the counterpart for the fifty miracle principles. (You can tell which side Jesus is on because he gives fifty miracle principles and only five laws of chaos.)

The first law of chaos is the exact counterpart to the first miracle principle. It states that truth is relative and that there is a hierarchy of illusions. Some illusions are worse than others, or some illusions are better than others. This, again, is exactly what we are talking about. Once you believe that certain problems are larger than others, you must believe there are different levels of solution for the different levels of the problem. Certainly, somebody who is in the medical field knows that if there is this symptom, you do "A," and if there is another symptom, you do "B," and if there is a third symptom, you do "A" *and* "B," or something else. They are all very specific things that we do to heal or solve the various problems that we believe we have. By the way, the Course makes it very clear that this does not mean that you should not do these various things, but I will elaborate on that later when it comes up with the miracle principles (see below, pp. 31f, 34).

The only thing that truly heals is undoing the belief that we are separate from God, which is where our problem of guilt comes from. As we will see later on, another way of saying what healing is would be "joining." If we recognize that the only problem that exists is the belief that we are separate, this must mean that the only solution to all other seeming problems is to join.

Another thing that will become apparent as we work with this material is that *A Course in Miracles* teaches that the way we define a problem automatically establishes how we resolve the problem. That is why it is very important in working with the Course that you always keep in mind that it recognizes only one problem, and that is the belief that we are separate. If you say that the problem is anything else, then you are automatically saying that the solution will be something else.

Workbook lesson 79 makes the point that there is only one problem, therefore there is only one solution. The one problem is guilt, separation, or holding grievances, and the one solution is a miracle, forgiveness, or joining. This first principle, then, really sets that up: "there is no order of difficulty in miracles." Regardless of what we believe the problem is, all our problems can be solved the exact same way, merely by changing our minds about them.

Q: Sometimes we deny things, and we think we have changed our minds already...

A: As it says right at the end of the text, "Trials are but lessons that you failed to learn presented once again, so where you made a faulty choice before you now can make a better one..." (text, p. 620; T-31.VIII.3:1). Obviously, most of the time we have not totally undone all our guilt, and there may be relationships that we believe we have healed and resolved and something happens a year later and, bang, all those same feelings just come surging back. Everyone has had that kind of experience.

This does not necessarily mean that we failed when we originally tried to work on it. What it probably means is that we went as far as we could go at that point, and then at some later point we were ready to take another step and heal a deeper layer of guilt. Then an opportunity presents itself and we find ourselves getting angry and upset, feeling hurt and victimized, and that is what tells us that we had not thoroughly let go of this belief, because what happens now is that it becomes projected out onto this person. The ego would tell us that we should believe that we are failures; what the Holy Spirit would tell us is that now we are ready to take another step. That is really the whole thrust of the Course: to help us look at everything that happens in our lives as an opportunity of healing and forgiving something that was deeply buried in us that we did not know was there. And there are no exceptions to that principle.

In fact, where the Course's great power comes from is that it is so consistent and simple in everything it says. It really teaches us only one way to look at everything in the world.

That is the way of *A Course in Miracles*: that everything that occurs is an opportunity for us to heal our minds, and it does not matter whether we get upset about some terrible event that we are reading about in the newspaper, or we get upset by a trivial thing that happens in our homes or our families, communities, or work situations.

Q: Although there may be no order of difficulty in miracles, we are pretty well convinced that there is anyway. In view of that fact, is it likely that we would need to experience forgiveness with a big issue before we get around to the other ones?

A: We work on whatever it is we can work on. Some people feel just the opposite, that the big ones are too much. So they practice on the little ones: the person who cuts you off on the highway, or someone who does a little annoying thing, or something that your kids may not do around the house that they are supposed to do. Some people find those easier to deal with than the larger issues, and other people feel just the opposite.

Q: Do you have to do all those things?

A: You do not have to, it is just that you would feel better if you do, that is all.

Q: Would the first principle also mean that it would be just as easy to have cancer cured as a cold?

A: Yes, but you can mistake the idea that the problem is the cancer or the cold of the body. That is not the problem. The problem is the thought that led to it. The Course says the only meaning of anything is what it is for. You do not focus on the symptom of the cancer any more than you would focus on the remission of the cancer, because that is not the problem. The cancer may serve a purpose, not only for that particular person, but for the people in that person's life—family, friends, medical people, etc.

Q: So that "there is no order of difficulty in miracles" never really means the cure of anything, it really means a change in perception.

A: Right, it means a change in mind. We will discuss that over and over again as we go through this.

Q: In line with that, if your thought has caused the cancerous condition and your mind does, in fact, become healed, does it not then be come irrelevant, whether or not the physical cancer is healed?

A: Right. People often use physical healing as a way of proving either their own spiritual or mental health, or the lack of it: "If I am really doing this right, then this tumor will disappear." And again, what it is doing is making this real. When your mind is really healed, it will not be a burning issue for you. It does not mean that the tumor will not disappear. It just means that your investment will not be in having it disappear. Your investment will be in having peace in your mind.

Q: Does not "death" mean that we just lie down and give up the body at the appropriate point?

A: If you mean by "appropriate" that we die when we have completed the lessons that we came to learn, yes. However, we may also change our mind and choose to leave our body before we have completed these lessons. As the Course says: "And no one dies without his own consent" (workbook, p. 274; W-pI. 152.1:4).

Q: To what degree does the shared perception of illness of those around us come into play? To what degree does that lock us into that perception, even though our mind is in the process of changing?

A: Within each of us there are always two voices. There is the ego's voice and the Holy Spirit's Voice. Most of the time we are going back and forth. Let us say that I am really practicing what *A Course in Miracles* is saying, but I am not totally practicing it. I still have some doubts or some fears, and you come along and other people come along and strongly reinforce the ego's way of looking. There is no question that that will strengthen my ego. If I were really firm, if I knew that everything the ego told me was false, then it would not matter how many people, thousands or millions, said something. I would know deep within me that it did not make any difference. But if I am wavering, then my ego will always be on the look-out for those people it can use as witnesses to reinforce its case. But the problem is not the people who are reinforcing it. The problem is that I am unconsciously looking for those witnesses that will prove that my ego is correct. As we all know, you do not have to look very far in the world. If you really want to prove that anger is justified, sickness is terrible, and separation is real, you will find witnesses all around you. As long as we are wavering, there is no question that other people's negative or ego thoughts will strengthen our own. They are not responsible for our own because that is like voodoo, the idea that you can influence someone else. The Course would never teach that, because that then puts the responsibility onto someone else. What *A Course in Miracles* would say is that other people's thoughts or what happens in the world can reinforce your own ego. But if you are really clear about what you believe, it will have no effect at all. Jesus, of course, would be the ultimate example.

Therefore, it is falling into the ego's trap to believe that smoking causes cancer; guilt does. But if you believe that smoking will hurt you, then you should not smoke. If you are diabetic, and the sickness still is part of your thought system, then not taking insulin would be an unconscious attempt to punish yourself, as would be eating ice cream, etc. In this context, then, taking care of your sick body would be the most loving and forgiving thing you could do.

Q: What does it mean to "hear" the Holy Spirit?

A: To speak of hearing the Holy Spirit is really a metaphor, just as it is to speak of Him as being God's Voice. The Holy Spirit communicates to us through our minds, and He will use any means or vehicle that we can accept. Thus, it can be what we call intuition, imagination, a sudden thought or insight, a dream, a feeling of words or thoughts coming to us that we "hear" and know are not our own. He is not fussy; He will use anything we give Him.

Let us move along, otherwise we will never get past the first line. The second line, of course, is just another way of saying what we have been talking about. To say that there are no "harder" or "bigger" miracles is the same thing as saying there are no harder or bigger problems. Bill Thetford used to say that the first principle could be restated as: There is no order of difficulty in problem solving. All problems are the same and, therefore, all the solutions are the same.

"All expressions of love are maximal." Most of you have probably heard me talk about the two levels that the Course is written on. The first is the metaphysical level, which is really not what we are spending much time on today. The second is the more practical level that contrasts the two ways of looking in the world. But the first level really is the part of the Course that does not have any compromise to it. Something is either all true or it is all false, and there is no in-between. You cannot be a little bit pregnant; you either are or you are not. On the second level, we go back and forth all the time between the ego and the Holy Spirit. But this statement, "all expressions of love are maximal," really is a Level One statement: You cannot have a little bit of love. You either have love or you do not have love, because one of the characteristics of love is that it is total, complete, and there are no exclusions to it, no exceptions. All expressions of love must be maximal, which is another way of saying that there is only one problem in the world. That problem is hatred or fear; and, therefore, there is only one solution for that problem, and that is love. Love does not come from us; it does not come from this world. Love comes from God, through the Holy Spirit Who then inspires us to be what we would call loving.

A Course in Miracles also teaches that no one in this world can be loving, because it says that love without ambivalence is impossible here (text, p. 55; T-4.III.4:6). The very fact that we are here means that we have an ego, which means that we believe in separation. This means we cannot believe in the all-inclusive nature of love. Technically, forgiveness is this world's equivalent of Heaven's love, and love comes to us from God through the Holy Spirit in our minds, Who then inspires all of the loving things that we would do. But here with the use of

18

the word "love" we can see how the Course is certainly not strict in its usage. Very often it will speak of love in terms of what we do here.

Q: What is he speaking of here then? If "all expressions of love are maximal," that would only apply to God's Love.

A: Yes, but God's Love through the Holy Spirit here. In other words, the context of the statement is the miracle. The miracle comes from love. The next principle talks about that.

Principle 2

Miracles as such do not matter. The only thing that matters is their Source, Which is far beyond evaluation.

The fact that "Source" is capitalized, of course, tells us that this is God, and God is present in our mind, in our split mind, through the Holy Spirit. What is important here also is to realize that miracles do not matter, because miracles are part of the same illusory world that the ego is. If the miracle is a correction, then it is a correction for an illusory thought, which also makes a miracle an illusion. It is needed only in a world of illusion. As we said earlier, you do not need a miracle in Heaven. You do not need forgiveness in Heaven. You need forgiveness or a miracle only in a place where you believe in sin, suffering, sacrifice, separation, etc.

The only thing that truly matters is God, or the creation of God, which is spirit, which is the Christ in us. In this world, however, miracles do matter, because that is the correction that enables us to remember eventually who we really are. The Course also speaks of forgiveness as an illusion. At one point it says it is the final illusion (workbook, p. 369; W-pI.198.3). What makes it different from all the other illusions in the world is that forgiveness is the end of illusion. All the other illusions here really breed illusions, so that they strengthen the illusion that we are separate or that attack is real and justified. Forgiveness is an illusion that teaches us that there are no illusions.

Q: If you say that we cannot obtain complete love in this life, how do we relate to Jesus?

A: Well, let me qualify that. I think there are very, very few exceptions, such as Jesus, who is the greatest symbol of God's Love. Furthermore, there are some people who have totally transcended their egos, and who stay around a while to help other people do that. They are what in the East are called avatars or bodhisattvas: people who have thoroughly transcended their ego yet remain, holding on to just a sliver of it so they can stay here in the body. They are no longer here to learn lessons. But as the Course implies at one point, this is such a rare occurrence that it does not pay to talk about it (manual, p. 61; M-26.2,3).

Q: What are our creations?

A: "Creations" is one of those technical words that the Course uses but does not really explain. What they refer to is the process of creation that we share with God. One of the basic attributes of spirit is that it is always extending itself. This is not a process that occurs in time or space, which is why it is so hard for us to conceive of it. God's extension of Himself—as spirit, He is always extending Himself—is what is called creation. We are the result of that, not we as we identify ourselves sitting here in this room, but the "we" that is the Christ that is all of us. Each of us is a part of that Christ which is an extension of God and, since Christ is part of God, He also shares in the basic attributes of God. One of those attributes is extension, so Christ also extends Himself. What Christ extends is what the Course calls "creations." Creations are really the extensions of us in our true state. Again, what makes it so difficult is that this process has no counterpart or referent to anything in this world. When the Course uses the word "create," as it will in one of these miracle principles, it does not refer to having a creative thought, to creating a work of art or anything like that—not that the Course would be against anything like that, it simply uses the word differently. "Create" is a word that *A Course in Miracles* always uses just to denote what spirit does. If you want to think along the lines of the traditional idea of the Trinity, the Second Person of the Trinity would consist not only of Christ, of which each of us is a part, but also the extensions of Christ, which are our creations.

Q: The Course seems to promise that our creations are waiting for us. Is that so?

A: Like a cheering squad. You are rushing home, and there they are on the sidelines, cheering you home. That is a metaphor, of course, the idea being that our own wholeness is continually calling to us to remember who we are.

In the last part of the second principle—that the Source is far beyond evaluation—"evaluation" is a word that belongs to this world. We are always evaluating, and the fact that we are evaluating something is, obviously, a process of judgment; it is a process of perception. If you are talking about evaluation, you are talking about an evaluator who evaluates something or someone else. So you are talking about separation: subject and object. Obviously, the whole process of evaluation has relevance only to the world of perception, which is not the world of God. God is beyond all evaluation because He is beyond judgment; He is beyond form; He is beyond separation; He is beyond perception. The miracle only matters to the extent that it teaches us that nothing here matters. Once we learn that lesson, then the use for the miracle is over. It is what the Course teaches about time: its only purpose is to teach us that there is no time (see below, pp. 60f). You can say the same thing about the world or the body: The only purpose that the world or the body has is to teach us that there is no world or body, but we cannot learn that without being here in the body. That is why *A Course in Miracles* very clearly teaches us that we should not deny our physical experiences here, or deny our body (text, p. 20; T-2.IV.3:8–11). It only says we should look at them differently.

Principle 3

Miracles occur naturally as expressions of love. The real miracle is the love that inspires them. In this sense everything that comes from love is a miracle.

Later on in Principle 32, Jesus says that he is the one who inspires miracles. I want to mention one thing about the role of Jesus and the role of the Holy Spirit, because in these principles they will be used interchangeably, and I will use them interchangeably. From the point of view of function, the Holy Spirit and Jesus are synonymous. They both serve the function of being the internal Teacher or the inner Voice that will lead us home. This makes sense when you consider that Jesus is the one who had totally transcended his ego, which means that the only Voice that he has within him is that of the Holy Spirit. *A Course in Miracles* teaches that we have two voices that are continually speaking inside us: the ego's voice and the Holy Spirit's Voice. Since Jesus no longer has an ego, the only voice that is within him is the Holy Spirit's Voice. That is why later on in the Course he says that he is the manifestation of the Holy Spirit (manual, p. 85; C-6.1:1). He is not the Holy Spirit, but the manifestation of the Holy Spirit. He also makes it clear in many references in the text how he had listened to the Holy Spirit (e.g., text, pp. 71, 75; T-5.II.9,10; T-5.IV.4:1). The Holy Spirit had been his Teacher, and now he will help us to learn the same lessons he did. Therefore, from the point of view of function, we could use the Holy Spirit and Jesus interchangeably. They both serve as the inner Voice, the internal Teacher who corrects the errors of the ego's teaching. The miracle, then, comes from him. To say that Jesus is the manifestation of the Holy Spirit is also to say he is the manifestation of God's Love.

In a more general sense, the real miracle is the love that inspires the miracle, which means that the real miracle, then, is God, or the Holy Spirit and Jesus Who speak for God inside our own minds. This also makes it clear, as these principles repeatedly do, that the miracle does not come from us. We are not the ones who could shift our perception from the ego to the miracle; that is the role of the Holy Spirit. All that we can do is to choose the miracle instead of the ego. That is what the Course refers to when it speaks of "the little willingness" (text, p. 355; T-18.IV). That is the only thing the Course requires of us: the little willingness that enables us to begin to question our judgment of the world, and of what we see in the world. It asks that we at least be able to question what we have made real in terms of our perceptions of other people or of ourselves. Again, it says "a little willingness"; it does not say a lot. It also teaches us that if we had a lot of willingness, then we would not need the Holy Spirit, the holy instant, or the Course (text, p. 355; T-18.IV.2,4,5).

Q: Would that be an expression of love?

A: Choosing to hear Jesus' voice rather than the ego would be. You could say that would be an expression of love or a decision for love. The idea really is to try not to get too hung up with the specific words, because then you will go crazy. This is not the Talmud. You are not supposed to dissect this and analyze this line by line in that sense. The idea is to use the words as a way of getting to what the experience is, which is an experience of God.

Remember, it is very easy to get trapped by words. The manual says that "words are but symbols of symbols. They are thus twice removed from reality" (manual, p. 51; M-21.1:9–10). *A Course in Miracles* speaks of God in symbolic terms, calling Him "Father," and often speaking of Him as having attributes of caring, loving, being lonely, etc. A section called "Beyond All Symbols" (text, p. 531; T-27.III) underscores the idea that truth and God are beyond all symbols and concepts we use here. Yet within this world, the Holy Spirit has need of symbols to lead us ultimately beyond them all. Right- and wrong-mindedness are the Holy Spirit's and the ego's use of symbols so that in this context the word "miracle" is used in a more general sense. Elsewhere, Principle 24 states: "*You* are a miracle."

Q: But the yardstick of always asking the question, "What is it for?"—is that one of the keys?

A: Yes, that *is* the key. As I alluded to before, the Course says the only thing we should ever ask of anything in this world is: "What is it *for*?" What purpose does it serve? (text, p. 341; T-17.VI.2:1–2) And there are only two purposes, just as we said there are only two contents. One is the purpose of the ego, which is to reinforce separation; the other is the purpose of the Holy Spirit, which is to heal the separation. That is why the Course repeatedly urges us, just as the gospel has done, not to judge. It is the ego that judges; and when we judge, we always judge based on form. One of the major ingredients in the ego system is judgment, because once you judge a form as being good or not good, sick or well, holy or not holy, you are making it real. You are saying that there are levels in this world, levels of holiness; there are some forms that are holier or better than other forms. If you have to pinpoint one of the major mistakes that organized religions have made, it is in the preoccupation with form, saying that form matters. Once you say that the form matters, then you are saying that the body is real. You are saying that there is a hierarchy of illusions: certain behaviors, certain bodies, certain forms are holier than others. What frees you from that temptation, again, is to ask the question, "What is it *for*?" It is the purpose that is holy, not the form. And what makes the purpose holy is that it comes from the Holy Spirit, which means that the purpose is to heal and to join. What makes something unholy is not the thing itself, not the form, not what it looks like, not what the behavior is, but the purpose that it serves: namely, to reinforce attack and separation. What the miracle does is correct that misperception; this will become clearer as we work through a lot of these other principles.

Principle 4

All miracles mean life, and God is the Giver of life. His Voice will direct you very specifically. You will be told all you need to know.

This is another way of saying that miracles come from love. They reflect the love of Heaven, and they obviously also reflect the life of Heaven, which has nothing to do with what we call life, which is life of the body, or life of the personality, all of which is really a part of the body. True life comes from God, and that is the life of the spirit which is immortal and eternal. It is the miracle that leads us back to God.

"His Voice," which is one of the Course's definitions for the Holy Spirit, "will direct you very specifically. You will be told all you need to know." One of the common questions that people ask is: "If the Course says you will be told very specifically, how come I do not hear specific answers?" I am sure everyone has that question and has that problem. One of the blocks to hearing the specific things that the Holy Spirit would tell us is that we demand that we hear them. Very often the questions that we ask of the Holy Spirit are really not questions; they are statements. We are really setting up a problem and then demanding that He answer it for us, which of course is just another expression of the arrogance of the ego believing that it knows what the problems are, and then it believes it knows what the answers are. But very often when we are asking God for help or praying for help, we are setting up the problem as we see it, and then asking Him to solve it for us and, of course, when He does not solve it, we believe we have an airtight case against Him: "You say you are going to answer me very specifically, and here I am. I am so honest and earnest and devout and faithful, and I do not hear anything." What we have really done, without being aware of it, is closed the door. It is not that the Holy Spirit is not speaking to us; it is that we cannot hear Him.

Q: Is that because in our minds we want the prayer answered our way?

A: Sure. At one point, the text speaks of the ego throwing a temper tantrum and screaming, "I want it thus!" (text, pp. 350f; T-18.II.4:1). We do that as children, but we also do it as adults. "This is how I want it." I remember that at times Helen used to make demands on Jesus and say, "This is nonnegotiable!" It never worked out well for her. Do not try that.

Also, remember that when the Course says that the Holy Spirit will tell us all we need to know, that He knows what we need to know better than we.

Q: Is this not only true in the sense that we consciously or subconsciously are expecting a certain kind of answer, but that we also define the problem?

A: Yes, that is what I mean. We set up the problem ourselves, and then we demand an answer to a problem we set up. The problem is that we are saying, "Here is what my problem is," rather than just basically saying, "I am not at peace, please help me be at peace." The true cause of not being at peace is that there is someone we are holding something against. There is some basic lack of forgiveness in ourselves, so the solution would always come in the form of some aspect of forgiveness, of joining with someone. Whether it is on a behavioral level or a thought level does not matter. Remember again, the key thing is recognizing that every single problem we believe we have in the world is an expression of unforgiveness.

One of my favorite lines from the Course, because it seems to make absolutely no sense at all, is the line that says, "Certain it is that all distress does not appear to be but unforgiveness" (workbook, p. 357; W-pI.193.4:1). Translated, it means that it is certain that all distress or problems do not appear to be what they really are. We believe distress comes from all the various kinds of problems we believe we have, but what really is happening is that the ego has dropped a smokescreen so we do not realize that every distress that we experience comes from a lack of forgiveness or a belief that we are separate. This means that the solution to every distress and every problem in our world—either our personal world or the world-at-large—would be to join and heal through forgiveness.

Q: Could you say something about the Holy Spirit and trust: that you just sort of sit and be still?

A: Yes, and then be aware and monitor your thoughts that are not still. One of the crucial parts of this process is that all we have to do is get ourselves out of the way. We do not have to do anything. The Introduction to the text says, "The Course does not aim at teaching the meaning of love, for that is beyond what can be taught. It does aim, however, at removing the blocks to the awareness of love's presence..." That is what the miracle does; it merely takes away the block that keeps from us the awareness that we are children of God. All that we are talking about with the miracle is that it undoes or corrects what the ego has done. It does not do anything; it undoes. The more that we can be still, which really means to let go of our ego, then to that extent we will hear more clearly whatever it is that we need to know.

Principle 5

Miracles are habits and should be involuntary. They should not be under conscious control. Consciously selected miracles can be misguided.

Basically, this means that the purpose of *A Course in Miracles* is to have us continually move away from our way of problem solving. One of the things we do is attack a problem; we define something a certain way and then we have answers for it. We are always working at it. The whole purpose of the Course is to train us to look at problems in a totally different way, and to help us have this become our immediate reaction more and more. In other words, for example, if we are in a situation and someone does something and we suddenly find ourselves getting upset or angry, more and more it should become a habit that we quickly turn within and ask for help to shift our perception of this person or situation. That is what is meant when the Course says that the miracle should be "involuntary," that we are not the ones who do it. One of the key ideas in *A Course in Miracles* which distinguishes it from many New Age systems that have a lot of similar ideas, is that the Course makes it very clear that we cannot do this on our own. We choose the miracles, but we are not the ones who do them. They cannot be done without the Holy Spirit's help. That is the meaning of "involuntary" and of "[miracles] should not be under conscious control." In Chapter 2 of the text, Jesus talks about the difference between his guidance and his control (text, p. 25; T-2.VI.1:3–8; 2:7–10). He says that we should turn over to him all of our thoughts of fear, our thoughts of separation, so that he can control them for us; then he can guide us. But, again, we should not try to do this on our own. We are not in charge—he is. It is our goal to become sufficiently healed so that Jesus thinks, speaks, and acts through us.

Also, the Course does not mean that we will not have problems in the world, or what we think of as problems. What it does mean is that we will be able to look at them differently. Our habitual response should be: What can I learn from this? What happens over time is that our reaction-time becomes shorter and shorter in terms of how long it takes us to correct our perceptions about what we believed was upsetting us.

Q: Can we use the word "alignment" with Jesus?

A: If you want to use the word "alignment," it would be in the sense that we align our thoughts with his, so that we begin to think like him. The whole Course is a training program, as it says at the end of the first chapter (text, p. 13; T-1.VII.4:1). It is a mind-training course, a way of training us to think absolutely differently from everything else. This is a very radical thought system. It teaches absolutely the opposite of everything the world believes, and it teaches the opposite of what many religious or spiritual systems believe, too. Let me mention, if I have not already, that *A Course in Miracles* makes it very clear that it is not the only path, that it is not the only form of truth. It just says that it is a path. The Course says of itself that it is one form among many thousands (manual, p. 3; M-1.4:1–2). But it is a specific path, which means that you really cannot combine it with anything else because it will not fit. The more that we explore what it is saying, the more we will recognize how radical it is.

What this principle is saying is that we should not trust our own perceptions and, therefore, that we should not choose how we should react to what we perceive. That is also what is meant by "consciously selected miracles can be misguided." Here it is using the word "miracle" in the popular sense of miracles being things that we do. It is saying, again, that we should not be the ones who choose what we do. We could be in the presence of someone who was suffering, and we might almost instinctively rush to do something to heal or take away that person's suffering, and that may not ultimately be the most loving thing to do. It may be coming out of pity; it may be coming out of guilt; it may be coming out of our own suffering; it may not be coming out of love. And so what Jesus is saying here is: "Do not consciously select what the loving act will be. Let me do that for you." This is a very clear point, and very important. A temptation that many people who work with the Course as well as people in other spiritual paths can fall into, is to be a kind of spiritual do-gooder. For example: you are going to bring peace to the world; you are going to bring people to the truth; you are going to help take away people's suffering, etc. All that you are really doing is making the suffering real because you are perceiving the suffering as outside. You also are not realizing that if you are seeing it outside, it must be only because you are seeing it within yourself. If you are perceiving someone else in pain, and you are identifying with that pain, it could only be because you are seeing it in yourself. It might be an example of reaction formation: I feel I am terrible and, therefore, I psychologically defend against my guilt by trying to help everyone else, atoning for my sin after having made my sin real.

This does not mean you deny what you see. If someone has broken his arm and he is screaming out in pain, it does not mean you deny that the person is feeling pain and turn your back on him. What it does mean is that you change how you look at that pain. You realize that the real pain is not from the body; the real pain is from the belief in separation in the mind. If you really want to be an instrument of healing, then you join with that person, which means, perhaps, that you rush the person to the hospital. But what you are really doing through the form of your behavior is joining with that person, and realizing that you are being healed as much as that person is.

The issue here is that this is not a decision we should make on our own. Very often when we try to help, we are really trying to do something else, which often is an extension of our own guilt. Pity is not a loving response. Sympathy is not a loving response. It sees you as different from the other person. In Chapter 16, the Course makes a distinction between false empathy and true empathy (text, p. 307; T-16.I). False empathy is identifying or empathizing with the person's body— whether we are talking about the physical body or psychological body—which means you are making the person weak by making the body real. True empathy is identifying with the strength of Christ in the person, realizing that this person's call for help is your call for help and, therefore, you are both joined beyond the body.

Remember, the key problem to watch out for is anything that reinforces separation. That is why the Course's view of healing is so different from what other paths call healing. Healing is not something that someone does. True healing, as *A Course in Miracles* sees it, does not come from saying a certain prayer, or by the laying on of hands, or by giving some people energy, or anything like that. If it did, you would be making something of the body real and saying you have a gift someone else does not have. That is not healing. This does not mean that these approaches cannot be helpful, nor does it mean that you should not use them. It just means that you should not call them healing, because then you would be reinforcing separation. Very subtly you would be making the body real.

The only real energy that is in this world is the Holy Spirit. Anything else in this world is a false energy, and is really of the ego, the body. The "healing energy of the world" is forgiveness, which comes from the Holy Spirit inside our minds. Any other form of energy may have relevance, existence, and reality within the world of the body, but that world of the body is inherently illusory. That is not what the Course is talking about in terms of healing. It is talking only about joining with the Holy Spirit in your mind by sharing His perception, thereby joining with other people.

Again, we are not the ones who can choose what it is we should do or what it is that we should not do. He is the one who chooses the expression of the miracle for us. Then He extends that miracle through us. Later on, the text amplifies this point, and says that our one concern is to bring our egos to

30

the Holy Spirit; the extension of forgiveness is not our responsibility (text, p. 449; T-22.VI.9:2–5). That is where we get tripped up. We try to extend the miracle ourselves, which just seems to be the loving or the holy thing. What we are very subtly doing is letting the arrogance of the ego take upon itself the role of God. Our responsibility is simply to ask for help to see something the way Jesus sees it rather than the way the ego sees it. That is our only responsibility. That is what the miracle is. Then he extends that miracle through us and specifically tells us what we should do or not do.

This is why there is often so much judgment and intolerance among religious and spiritual paths. Guilt was never truly forgiven, but was simply repressed and then projected out in the form of religious self-righteousness. I remember an example of this many years ago, shortly after *A Course in Miracles* was published. We met a man who had prepared a long chart of the Course's corrections of the Bible which he was about to present to several ministers he knew, showing them what Jesus really taught. Basically, what he was doing was hitting the traditional churches over the head with the Course, just as he believed he had been hit over the head with the Bible. Fortunately, we were able to stop him in time. The whole point is that we should be sensitive to what is going on inside our own minds, be aware of anything in our thinking that would cause us to be separate from others, recognizing that this must be our ego. We should always be cautious of judging according to form, which, of course, is the ego's only way of judging. Yet, it is nonetheless true that within the illusory world some people are more advanced than others—Jesus being the extreme example—however, we must always be careful of judging.

Q: I am finding this very difficult. As a nurse, I am supposed to respond to pain and suffering, and I pray that in emergency situations I do the right thing.

A: That is basically what I am talking about. This does not mean, by the way, that if you are a nurse and someone comes rushing in and is bleeding to death, you say, "Oh, hold it a moment; I have to go and meditate and ask what I should do." That is really not a loving thing. You basically assume that you want to do the right thing; you want Jesus to act through you, and then you just act. If I am seeing people in my office, I do not stop every fifteen minutes and say, "Hold it, I have to check in with the Boss before I can tell you what to do or what I think." I just naturally trust that my reactions or what I say will come from Jesus rather than my ego. What I then try to do is always monitor my own feelings and thoughts, so that if I feel something that I know is coming from my ego and not from him, at that point I ask his help that that be taken out of the way. I do not focus on what I say, because if I did I would always be tripping over my words and I could not say anything. My focus is not on what I say, but on getting myself out of the way.

Q: That is the thing with laying on of hands and praying for someone who has an illness.

A: That does not mean you should not do that...

Q: Is that reinforcing, though?

A: No. It depends on why you do it. In other words, if you find that people can be helped by your laying on of hands, then there is nothing wrong with your doing that as long as you realize that that is just a form through which the Holy Spirit is joining you with someone else, and that the healing is not coming because of the laying on of hands. I mean, what happens if your hands are broken, or you are a quadriplegic? Does that mean you cannot heal? No, it is not the form; it is the meaning that you give the form.

Let me read something from the section, "Healing as Release from Fear" (text, p. 19; T-2.IV), that specifically talks about the difference between magic and healing. Anything that is of the body is magic. Anything that we do on this level to help solve a problem is magic because it is seeing the problem in the body, and then applying the remedy to the body. This holds whether you are talking about traditional medicine, New Age forms of medicine, laying on of hands, or saying prayers. They are all part or forms of magic. But then it says that this does not mean that all this is sinful. The last paragraph on page 20 (text, p. 20; T-2.IV. 5:1) states, "The value of the Atonement does not lie in the manner in which it is expressed." The "Atonement," which we will talk about a little later, is the Course's word for the correction of the ego, which means that the principle of the Atonement refers to joining, because the ego is based on separation. What we are saying is that the value of the Atonement, the principle of joining, does not lie in the manner in which it is expressed. "In fact, if it is used truly, it will inevitably be expressed in whatever way is most helpful to the receiver. This means that a miracle, to attain its full efficacy, must be expressed in a language that the recipient can understand without fear" (text, p. 20; T-2.IV. 5:2–3).

If people come to you and believe that by your laying on of hands they can be healed, then of course you should do that. Just as, if I come to a surgeon and believe that by this person cutting open my body and taking out this or that I will feel better, then, yes, of course I should do that. If people believe that by your saying a specific prayer they will be helped, then of course you should do that. But what the Course would say is just recognize that what you are doing has nothing to do with the form, because a form limits. What it has to do with is the underlying meaning of what you do: joining with people. As this passage says, the Holy Spirit does not care about the way you join. Since we live in a world of symbols and we live in a world of bodies, we have to use the symbols and we have to use our bodies. As it says in "The Song of Prayer" (a pamphlet that Helen had scribed after the Course): it is a mistake to believe that you have some healing gifts that others, such as spiritual healers and physicians, do not have (pp. 17f).*

This does not mean you should stop doing whatever it is that you are doing. That probably is not what the Holy Spirit would be asking you to do. All that He would be saying is stop thinking that the form of what you are doing has any healing properties whatsoever, because once you do that you are saying

---

*"The Song of Prayer: Prayer, Forgiveness, Healing" (Glen Ellen, CA: Foundation for Inner Peace, 1978)

that there is something of this world that is real; there is power in a word. There cannot be any power in a word. A word is made up. As I said before, the Course says that "words are but symbols of symbols. They are thus twice removed from reality" (manual, p. 51; M-21.1:9–10).

Krishnamurti worked out a very clever way of making this point. He said that if you want to make something holy, do a little experiment. Put whatever the object is on your mantelpiece, and every day for thirty days go before it. Bring it flowers, put incense around it, say a little phrase. It could be "Shalom"; it could be "Coca Cola"; it could be whatever your favorite mantra is. At the end of thirty days, that object will become holy for you, not because there is any inherent holiness in the object, but because you have given it the holiness by believing it is holy.

That is why this idea is so central to the Course's thought system. There is absolutely nothing in this world that has holiness attached to it, because there is nothing in this world. It is all a product of what is in our mind. If we believe something is holy, then it will become holy for us. If we feel there is a certain power coming from a person or from a thing in the world, it is because we have put that power there. The one power in this world is universal, and that is the power of Christ which is inside each of us. We all share in that power equally. Once you believe there are certain things in this world that are holier or more powerful than others, or certain people who are holier or more powerful than others, you are saying there is a hierarchy of illusions. That, again, is the first law of chaos (text, p. 455; T-23.II.2:3).

That is why that is the first law of chaos, because all the other laws rest upon that one. This also applies to A Course in Miracles. The only thing that is holy about this book is that it can lead you closer to God, but that could be said about anything. The book itself is not inherently holy. Sometimes people come to approach this book with reverence and almost genuflect in front of it, and feel it and touch it. There is nothing wrong in doing that. Often it seems kind of sweet, but they are really projecting something in their mind onto the book.

There is nothing in this world, the world of form, that means anything. That is the purpose of the early workbook lessons which say that nothing in this world means anything. What is really being said is that the only meaning something can have is the meaning that you give it. If it is the ego in you giving it meaning, then it is meaningless. If it is the Holy Spirit in you giving it meaning, then it is meaningful. Again, this does not mean you should give up whatever specific forms in this world work for you. That is not what *A Course in Miracles* is saying. All it is saying is: just realize that the reason the form is working is that you believe in it; and therefore it may be the way that Jesus or the Holy Spirit is using to help you recognize what the true Source of all meaning is, which is God. That is what the miracle does—it shifts the misbelief of the ego that there is something real out here, either a problem or the solution, and it teaches us that the only thing that is real is the use that we give it, and that use comes from God. Everything in the world, then, can be used to bring us closer to Him.

Q: You need to clarify that for me.

A: It is very easy to go off on this point. A lot of people work with *A Course in Miracles* and misunderstand what this is saying. To say that magic is not healing is not to say that magic is evil, or magic is sinful. In this world you cannot avoid magic. Magic is anything that is on the level of the world. This Course, then, is magic. What changes it to a miracle is the purpose you give it.

Q: Sunset, sunrise, and you are not real? Are they not God's creation?

A: No. The only thing that is real about a sunset is that the Holy Spirit can use it as a way of helping you draw closer to God. But the sunset itself is inherently illusory. What makes the sunset? Colors? God did not create the sunset, or the sun, or the world. The Course's basic teaching is that the ego made the world. We put it there. Some things we did, we did pretty well. We did okay with sunsets and sunrises; we did not do okay with scorching suns that kill people. We did well with gentle rains that make the grass grow; but we really fluffed it with hurricanes and floods. Everything in this world is a two-edged

35

sword, you see, which the Course teaches is how you know God could not have created it.

Basically, the principle is that God, being spirit, could only extend or create what is like Him. He could not have created the body or the form which is not like Him. That came from the ego: the body is the projection of the thought that we are separate.

Q: Was there ego before body?

A: Yes. There was a thought of separation and a belief that we could be separate from God. That is the ego. When the thought of separation became projected out of the mind, the world and the body arose.

Principle 6

Miracles are natural. When they do not occur something has gone wrong.

The Course teaches us that the most natural thing in this world is to be at peace and one with God, because that peace comes from the Holy Spirit within us. The unnatural things in this world are those that defend against that naturalness: feelings of anger, conflict, depression, loss, guilt, anxiety, etc. All these are not natural, because they do not come from who we really are. In this world, feelings of peace, joy, and being one with people do reflect who we really are and, therefore, they are natural.

In other words, when miracles do not occur, and here we can think of a miracle as the extension of the Holy Spirit within our minds, something has gone wrong because we have put something in the way. That is all the ego is: an obstruction that keeps from us the awareness of who we really are.

Q: I was having a problem before with your comment that no one is holier, and I think what you just said made sense. With some people you just experience a presence, a wholesomeness, in that they are one with themselves or God and, therefore, I guess that is what I would call a holy person.

A: What that means is that they have fewer impediments to their holiness than other people do. In this world, that is true. Later on in this chapter, which we are not going to cover today, Jesus speaks of himself and says that he is no different from anyone else (text, p. 5; T-1.II.3:5–6). He is not any holier or less holy than anyone else. The only difference is that he got through his ego faster than the rest of us. In the world of time, he is different from us because he has no ego. In the world of eternity, however, he is the same as we are. That is why he says that to experience him in awe is a mistake, because he defines awe as something that is justified only when you are in the presence of someone who is greater than you. The only Person with Whom that is justified, then, is God, because God is our Creator. We should not be in awe of Jesus, because he is our equal. He is just a little bit smarter than we are, that is all. Therefore, we should ask him for help.

Q: To take that a little further, in everything that we see and apprehend in other people, that we think is holy, are we seeing our own holiness?

A: Yes, but you have to be very careful. Very often when we see how this person is really holy, what we are very subtly doing is putting ourselves down. We are saying this person is holier than I am. Almost always that is what we are doing. That is the mistake. That is why, from the point of view of the Course, the mistake that made Jesus greater than anybody else occurred. It was not a way of making Jesus greater; it was a way of making ourselves smaller, saying that he is the only Son of God. It was a way of saying he is perfect and pure, which really was a way of expressing the fact that people felt so impure. It was not so much a statement about Jesus, it was a statement about what was in ourselves. We felt so guilty and sinful we had to make him different. And the whole point of his teaching is that we are not different; we are all the same. We are all Christ.

The only difference with Jesus is that he was the first one who recognized who he really was, that he was Christ, and that he helps everyone else recognize that they are also Christ. An example of what the Course would call "spiritual specialness"

37

is our making certain people better or more holy or more spiritual than others. Very subtly what that does is put ourselves down, which means that we reinforce the belief that we are separate. The same thing is true when we think we are more spiritual than someone else—opposite sides of the same coin.

Principle 7

Miracles are everyone's right, but purification is necessary first.

"Purification" is not a word that is frequently used in the Course. It is certainly a word that has more connotations in Judaism and Christianity, which is why I think it appeared here. The earliest sections and chapters in the Course, in particular, use biblical references to a great extent because Helen knew the Bible rather well, especially the New Testament, and it was a way of Jesus helping her bridge a gap. What *A Course in Miracles* means by "purification" is nothing that you do with the body.

Q: You say Helen knew the Bible, especially the New Testament, because she studied it?

A: Why did she know it? She liked reading it. She liked the way it was written. She always had a wonderful sense of style and language. She had a love-hate relationship with Christianity, and the Catholic Church especially, but there was a part of her that was very much attracted to it, as well as to the New Testament. She could quote whole passages. She was also very familiar with the dogmas, doctrines, and teachings of the Catholic and mainstream Protestant Churches. But she never formally studied the Bible.

"Purification," as the Course uses it, has nothing to do with the body. You do not purify a body or deprive a body, because the body is not impure. If the body is inherently an illusion, as *A Course in Miracles* teaches, then there is nothing you have to do with the body. What makes the body sinful, impure, or unholy, are our thoughts, which means it is our thoughts that have to be purified, not the body. That is why it would certainly not be the Course's method to do anything with the body. Asceticism could not be the Course's form of spirituality, for asceticism's purpose is to purify the body. The Course's idea is that you purify the mind. As St. Augustine said, "Love and do what you will." If love is in your heart and in your mind, then everything you do will be an extension of that love. Therefore, you do not have to worry about the body; that is worrying about the wrong thing. That is not where the problem is. What you worry about are the thoughts in your mind. The one thought that has to be healed is the thought of guilt; that is what has to be purified. So, when the Course says that miracles are everyone's right—it is saying that miracles are for all of us.

Another important implication here is that miracles are not things that certain people do. One of the big mistakes that formal religions make is to ascribe certain spiritual powers or properties to some people and not others. There are some people who can work miracles and not others; these are the holy people. These are the people who have been chosen by the various religious institutions as being able to do certain things that everyone else cannot do. What the Course is saying here is that miracles are something that we can do; in fact, we all should do. A miracle is not parting the Red Sea or walking on water; the miracle is shifting from the ego's perception to the Holy Spirit's. That is what the miracle is; and this is everyone's right. This then means that any person can be the instrument for the Holy Spirit or Jesus, extending Their Love through him or her in whatever form is the most helpful and most loving. Our focus, then, is not on the external miracle. Our focus is on purifying the impediments to this miracle, on removing the obstacles to the awareness of love's presence. What has to be purified are our thoughts of separation, our thoughts of guilt. What purifies them for us is asking the Holy Spirit to forgive through us.

Q: How would you judge or measure progress in the Course?

A: I would not try to measure anyone's progress except my own, and that progress would just be the extent of peace I feel.

Each of us would have within our own lives a beautiful way of measuring that. In other words, if you are in a situation that five weeks ago or five years ago drove you up a wall, or you are in the presence of someone who filled you with instant hate or instant fear, and suddenly you could be with that person and feel at peace, that would be an indication that you are doing all right. It is always a real mistake to try to judge another person. There is a line in the text which says that what we judge to be our greatest successes have been our greatest failures, and what we have judged to be our greatest retreats have been our greatest advances (text, p. 357; T-18.V.1:6), which is a nice, gentle way of Jesus telling us that we do not know what is going on. And if we do not know what is going on in ourselves, how are we supposed to know what is going on in anyone else?

Principle 8

Miracles are healing because they supply a lack; they are performed by those who temporarily have more for those who temporarily have less.

Principle 8 introduces the word "lack," which is a word that *A Course in Miracles* uses from time to time and is part of the concept of the "scarcity principle." This is that aspect of our guilt that teaches us that there is something missing in us, or there is something scarce. Of course, the ego never tells us that what is missing is God. God is excluded from the ego system, and that is what the Course means by the "scarcity principle." Lack is just the derivative of that. The belief that there is something lacking comes from the ego belief or perception of the world, which is a world of separation. This is now talking about how the miracle becomes the correction for that belief in lack. The miracle teaches us that we are not separate from each other, that we are really one with each other. That, of course, becomes a reflection of the wholeness of Christ. The miracle removes the burden of guilt that keeps us from remembering the abundance of Christ.

The principle states: "Miracles are healing because they supply a lack." This is another indication of how the Course is not precise with its language. Basically, as it says elsewhere, you do not "supply a lack," because that really means that there is a lack that you then fill up, which would be making the lack real. The more correct way of stating it, which is really how the Course speaks of it later on, is that it corrects the misperception of lack. That is what the miracle does.

"They are performed by those who temporarily have more for those who temporarily have less" means that the miracle is done by someone who is in his right mind, as opposed to the person who temporarily has less who is in his wrong mind. That is really what those words mean. The word "temporarily" is important here. A passage in the text talks about how healing occurs when the healer is without fear (text, p. 535; T-27.V.2:7-14). However, this does not mean that the healer is always without fear; only in the instant when he chooses to heal instead of to attack. We go back and forth all the time. The pamphlet on psychotherapy says that the therapist should be one or two steps ahead of his patient (p. 7).* As any therapist knows, this is not always the case, and it certainly does not mean miles ahead. Once again, "miracle" here is used in the sense of something that someone does: it is performed. That is the popular use of the word "miracle."

Principle 9

Miracles are a kind of exchange. Like all expressions of love, which are always miraculous in the true sense, the exchange reverses the physical laws. They bring more love both to the giver *and* the receiver.

The ego's understanding of giving is that when I give you something, I no longer have it. If I give you something, you have more of it and I have less of it. Giving, to the ego, is always quantitative. Now, this is so whether we are talking

---

*"Psychotherapy: Purpose, Process and Practice" (Glen Ellen, CA: Foundation for Inner Peace, 1976).

about material things, or we are talking about psychological things or thoughts. One of the key aspects of projection is that by my giving you my guilt I am free of it, and you have it. We always believe that when we give a thought away, then someone else has it and we do not have it.

The miracle corrects that and teaches us that what we give we also receive, since we are all one. Since I am really not giving anything that is out here, because there is nothing out here, it is all in my mind. Giving, then, is really a reinforcement. If I give you my guilt by projecting it onto you and attacking you, what I am really doing is reinforcing my own guilt. If I give you love, then what I am doing is reinforcing the fact that there is a Presence of Love Who is within me, and that Presence, the Holy Spirit, is the One Who is really giving the love. That is why what we give away we really receive. Giving and receiving are the same. That is one of the key principles found in the material. Several workbook lessons have that as their basic idea (e.g., lessons 108, 126), and certainly the text discusses it over and over again.

Miracles, then, become an exchange. I allow the Holy Spirit to extend His Love through me, which not only reinforces who you are, as a child of love, but it also reinforces who I am, healing both of us.

That idea is a reversal of how the world thinks or the ego thinks, and that is what the statement means. It reverses the physical laws because the world teaches, again, that what we give away we have less of, so that the more miracles we choose, and the more we can allow ourselves to be the instruments of the miracle, the more we receive the benefits of the miracle. The more that we love, heal, and forgive, the more loved, healed, and forgiven we become. The St. Francis Prayer is a lovely expression of that principle.

Principle 10

The use of miracles as spectacles to induce belief is a misunderstanding of their purpose.

Here, too, the word "miracle" is used in the popular sense of people doing miracles. I think we could translate that in terms of doing things for other people so that we would look good, or it could also be understood as people who have what we refer to as psychic ability who in a sense show off. That lets the world know that they are better than other people, or they have some gift that other people do not have, that they are holier, wiser, better, etc. All that is happening, then, is that we are using our abilities or gifts to serve the ego's purpose rather than the Holy Spirit's.

Q: In the case of a visible, physical healing, an act of genuine love rather than another ego expression, is the form in which it expresses or manifests itself still not the miracle?

A: Right. The miracle is the joining in your own mind. You can say it is the effect of the miracle, but the miracle is only something that happens in the mind, because that is the only place that there is a problem. The miracle is the decision to join with the Holy Spirit and thereby join with that other person. What happens after that you could call the effect of the miracle.

This is a very important distinction. Otherwise, there is a danger of becoming too invested in the externals—the seeming effects of the miracle. And then, when they do not happen, we feel something has gone wrong, and even more important, that we have gone wrong: we are failures. This is a real trap that healers in the world can fall into. They develop special relationships with those they are trying to heal; they become dependent on them for their own sense of self-worth. This is why, for example, psychiatrists are said to have the highest suicide rate of any professional group. If their patients do not get better, as they would judge "better"—and people have a way of not doing what we would like them to do—then they have failed. After a while, the burden of this "failure" becomes too heavy and the only way out is suicide.

Principle 11

Prayer is the medium of miracles. It is a means of communication of the created with the Creator. Through prayer love is received, and through miracles love is expressed.

This principle introduces the idea of prayer, a word not often used in the Course. Usually, the Course's treatment of prayer has to do with the idea of petition, of praying for something or praying for someone. That is usually the way that *A Course in Miracles* uses the word "prayer" and, as it says later on in the text, the only meaningful prayer is for forgiveness because you have everything else (text, p. 40; T-3.V.6:3). Once you pray to God for something to happen on the level of the body, whether it is your body or another person's body, you are making the body and the world real, which means you are falling into the ego's trap. As we saw earlier, you are then basically telling God what He should do. You are telling God, "This is my problem," or "This is what I want You to take care of, and now I am expecting You to do so." That is just another example of the arrogance of the ego which usurps the place of God.

So when the Course says "the only meaningful prayer is for forgiveness," it is saying that the only thing we should ever pray for is that our minds be healed from the ego's way of thinking to the Holy Spirit's way of thinking. In effect, that is what our little willingness does. It is a way of praying to the Holy Spirit for help that we share His perception of the world rather than our own.

The Holy Spirit does not have to be told where He should extend His miracle or His Love in the world. All that is necessary is that we get ourselves out of the way, which is what forgiveness does, so that He can then work through us and use us as His instruments. The pamphlet "The Song of Prayer" uses the analogy of prayer as a ladder, and the highest rung on that ladder is what we would call mystical prayer, or prayer as an experience of communion with God. All the earlier rungs are the steps towards that experience. It begins with the idea of praying for things or praying for other people, and progresses through that, recognizing that we do not pray for others; we really pray for ourselves. But, almost always, when the Course uses the word "prayer," it is using it in the way that traditional religion has—as praying for things—and, obviously, it has a different way of looking at that.

Here, however, when it talks about prayer, it is reflecting that top rung of the ladder, which would be an experience of having joined with God through the Holy Spirit. In that sense, then, prayer becomes the "medium of miracles." It is aligning our wills with that of Jesus or the Holy Spirit that allows their miracle to work through us.

Basically, only in this first chapter does *A Course in Miracles* talk about revelation, which is expressed here when it talks about prayer as "a means of communication of the created with the Creator." The Course makes a distinction between revelation and the miracle—that revelation is a temporary experience of oneness with God, which is not the goal of the Course. This is why it really does not discuss it afterwards. Revelation is in contrast with the miracle, the experience of joining with the Holy Spirit that thereby joins us with everyone else. "Revelation unites you directly with God. Miracles unite you directly with your brother" (text, pp. 4f; T-1.II.1:5-6). If a person has a revelatory experience, that is all well and good, but that is not the thrust of the Course.

"Through prayer love is received, and through miracles love is expressed." What is being discussed here is the experience of feeling God's Love and then letting the Holy Spirit take that Love and extend it through us. The goal of this, therefore, is to let ourselves become purified of any of the things that would hinder the Holy Spirit's using us as a channel for His Love.

Q: What about the prayers at the end of the workbook, all addressed to God the Father?

A: That is another example of the Course's inconsistency on the level of language or expression. Elsewhere, as we know, *A Course in Miracles* makes it very clear that God does not even know about this world, the dream of the sleeping Son that is outside His Mind. So, it would not make too much sense, on that level, to pray to Him. But the Course is not rigidly adhering to a form of expression. What it is really doing here is using "God" as a metaphor for the Holy Spirit, who is His Voice. You will find the same thing at the very end of "The Song of Prayer," where the first person is God Himself. So, really, the Course is giving the reader a choice in terms of form, whether you ask help of God, the Holy Spirit, Christ, Jesus, or anyone else you might feel comfortable with—it does not matter.

Principle 12

Miracles are thoughts. Thoughts can represent the lower or bodily level of experience, or the higher or spiritual level of experience. One makes the physical, and the other creates the spiritual.

This is a very important principle. It says "Miracles are thoughts," so a miracle is a change from the ego's thought to the Holy Spirit's thought. Miracles are thoughts because everything is thought. Nothing has existence outside our minds. The miracle is the thought that corrects or undoes the ego's thought of separation.

This principle is another example of what I earlier referred to as Level One. The Course can be understood on two different levels: Level One and Level Two. Level One is the basic metaphysical foundation for the Course's thought system. Everything is either true or false; everything is either of God or of the ego and there is no in-between, no compromise. Level Two is that part of the Course's system that deals with this physical world, where the distinction is made between the ego's way of looking and the Holy Spirit's way of looking.

What is being talked about in this principle is Level One, that there are two kinds of thoughts: the ego thoughts, and basically it is those ego thoughts that made up this world, and the Holy Spirit's thoughts. This is the first time in this material that you find the distinction between the words "make" and "create." Spirit creates and the ego makes. Later on in the text, this is explained in more detail (text, pp. 39f; T-3.V.2,3). When the word "create" is used, it is only used to denote the activity of spirit, and that has nothing to do with, and no counterpart to, anything in this world. On this Level, which again is Level One, our thoughts can either be of the spirit, which means that they create, or they can be of the ego, which means that they make.

There are two kinds of making, what I call Level Two, which are really not what is being talked about here. One is the ego's wrong-minded making, which is that it not only made up the world, but then it made up a thought system and a way of being in this world that reinforces the separation. Or, we could have thoughts of the right-minded part of our split minds which come from the Holy Spirit, which undo the separation of the ego. Basically, all that we are talking about is that there are two ways of being in this world: one is the ego's, and one is the Holy Spirit's. Both of those ways are illusory, because they both operate within this framework. The crucial idea is that "miracles are thoughts," that they are corrective thoughts to take the place of the thoughts of the ego. We can also say that miracles reflect the principle of creation or extension of spirit in Heaven. Yet, they themselves are illusions because they come within the world of illusion and, thus, correct what never was.

Principle 13

Miracles are both beginnings and endings, and so they alter the temporal order. They are always affirmations of rebirth, which seem to go back but really go forward. They undo the past in the present, and thus release the future.

The best way of understanding this is in terms of this diagram on the board (see next page). We can think of this path as a carpet that reflects the entire span of our experience in this world. What the miracle does is take certain aspects of this experience, all of which are predicated on the belief in separation or on our guilt (here is where the beginning and the ending would come from), and in a sense, isolates them as problem areas that we have to deal with.

The Carpet of Time

GOD CHRIST	real world happy dream	ego - guilt ⟶
		world - body - form - time
		⟵ Holy Spirit - forgiveness

Let us say that we are having a particular difficulty in a relationship. The miracle would cause us to focus on that relationship and to forgive it. In that sense, the miracle will be a beginning and an end because it circumscribes what the problem is. When we heal the problem, which means we forgive the one person who has been the greatest difficulty for us, or when we truly let go of a situation that has brought about tremendous feelings of separation, anxiety, guilt, anger, etc., what happens then is that this whole aspect of time has been shrunk. That is what is meant by saying that miracles "alter the temporal order."

The Course teaches that when the separation began, in that one instant, all of time, the entire world of evolution occurred at the same time. In that one instant that we believed that we had separated from God, a huge carpet spun out. This is the carpet that would constitute the entire world of evolution— past, present, and future.

A Course in Miracles also teaches that in that same instant that seemed to occur, God created the Holy Spirit, Who undid the very belief that gave rise to this carpet. It is like the separation occurred in an instant, and in that same instant it was corrected. The problem is, however, that we still believe that this world of time and space that we are living in, which really is a dream, is reality. That is why the Course speaks of the Holy Spirit as a Voice. He is God's Voice Who extends into the dream so that He can awaken us from the dream, and the entire world of evolution is all part of this dream.

One of the ways that the ego has rooted us in this dream, into believing that the dream is reality, is that it has made up the notion of time as linear: past, present, and future. This is the key stumbling block in trying to understand how the Course sees time and how the miracle operates. Our minds are so structured in the belief that time is linear that it is impossible for us to recognize that time is really holographic, which is a model that quantum physics has given us. Holography teaches that within each part of something is contained the whole, which means that within each of our minds, despite what we consciously believe, is the entire history of the ego, which is the entire history of not only this planet, but the entire physical universe. What makes this such a mind-boggling concept is that the mind (and therefore the brain) has been so severely limited by the construct of time that we made up, which is a linear view: past, present, and future.

What really happens is that at any given moment we choose to experience a particular part of this hologram; we dip into our mind and choose to go through or experience a part of this entire dream. That is what the Course means when it says that we walk through a script that is already written (workbook, p. 291; W-pI.158.3,4). This is the script. The Holy Spirit does not write the script. The Holy Spirit does not cause things to happen to us in the world. What the Holy Spirit does do is join with us in this script and teach us there is another way of looking at it. There is a line in the workbook where the Course speaks of the Holy Spirit as the One "Who wrote salvation's script in His Creator's Name" (workbook, p. 316; W-pI.169.9:3).

Salvation's script is the ego script turned around. Where the ego script had as its purpose to reinforce the belief in separation, the Holy Spirit uses that script, which means all the relationships and situations in our experience, so that we can learn that we are not separate. He uses the world as a classroom; the ego uses the world as a prison. It is the same world, but the ego's way of looking at it roots us even further in it. The Holy Spirit's way of looking at it releases us from it.

What keeps us on this carpet is guilt, which means that the way that we awaken from this dream, or get off the carpet, is to be free of this guilt. That is what forgiveness does. The one claim that the Course makes for itself is that it will save time. It says this repeatedly. For example, Jesus tells us that if we do what he says, it will save us time (text, p. 363; T-18.VII.4–6), and many times he says we can save a thousand years (e.g., text, p. 6; T-1.II.6:7).

A Course in Miracles does not specifically talk about the issue of reincarnation or past lives, except in one place, and there it does not take a stand (manual, p. 57; M-24.3:1). It certainly does imply in many references, however, that this is not the first time that we have come. When it says that we could save a thousand years, it is really saying that we could save many, many lifetimes. This then means that if we have a huge problem of guilt that we have expressed in a certain area of our relationships, there is something that we are continually doing that reinforces our own hatred of ourselves and our own belief in separation. In the ordinary span of time, it may take us ten lifetimes to work that through, to keep coming back over and over again until we have worked that through. If, however, we choose to work this difficult problem out, which means, usually, a relationship or situation that the world would judge as being very heavy, filled with a lot of pain, anguish, and suffering, and we could really look at it differently, which basically means realize that we are not victims of this other person or victims of ourselves, then in one lifetime we could just take this problem and erase it. That is what the Course means by saying we could save time or we could save a thousand years. That is what it means when it says of the miracle that it abolishes time, or it "alters the temporal order." It does not abolish the whole span of time; that it does not do. What it does do is collapse the amount of time it would have taken us to work through the huge problem of guilt we have.

It is not necessary, certainly, to understand or even agree with this whole metaphysical view of time. What is necessary is to realize, when you find yourself in a very difficult and painful situation, that there is a purpose that you could identify within that situation. The purpose is that you could learn not to see yourself as a victim, and to the extent that you learn that, to that extent you will heal all this guilt in yourself. That is what saves you time.

Q: I understand what you are saying, but it is hard to view this in terms of the collective ego, of which there are many parts. Some parts of this ego are on their way back, rolling up the carpet, and some are rolling it out farther. It is like one step forward and two backwards. How does this carpet ever get rolled back?

A: The Course says that "the outcome is as certain as God" (text, pp. 18, 52; T-2.III.3:10; T-4.II.5:8). I think that within the illusion it would take a long, long time. As the Course teaches, there is a tremendous amount of fear in this world.

Q: It perpetuates itself.

A: It seems to. When Helen first started receiving this material from Jesus, he gave her a brief explanation of what was happening. He described the terrible situation that the world seemed to be in, and he said that there was a celestial speed-up. He said that people were being asked to come back into the world to lend their talents on behalf of this plan as a way of helping others change their minds more quickly. *A Course in Miracles* would be one of the parts of the plan. Helen and Bill played their role in bringing it into the world to help people change their minds more quickly. Also, the Course fits in perfectly with the age in which we now live, an age still dominated by a Christianity that is not very Christian, despite many of the radical changes of the last twenty years, and an age of psychology. Above all, it is an age wherein we have gotten far away from the sane idea that salvation does not lie in attack, and much more insane in terms of believing that separate interests—both personally and internationally—are the way out of hell. Moreover, we live in an age that seriously questions the values of our authorities—political, religious, scientific, social, educational, etc.—and so would be relatively open to new ideas. Because of this, many would see *A Course in Miracles* as part of the New Age, although in its message it far transcends New Age thought and is more a part of the great ancient traditions of spirituality.

Q: But if time does not exist, why would it be necessary to speed things up?

A: That is true. However, suppose your child is having a nightmare. You know it is a nightmare, but within the nightmare your child is still suffering. So, as a parent you would want to diminish your child's suffering, even though you know it is not real. That is basically the way that the Holy Spirit would look at it, or Jesus would look at it. It is not that our pain is real, but that we believe it is real, and so this is a way of helping us out of our pain.

Q: Can you say something about where guilt comes from?

A: The basic source of guilt is our believing that we attacked God and separated from Him. That is what the Course means by sin, and certainly is the same idea as original sin. From the belief that we attacked God and separated from Him we will feel guilt, and guilt is a psychological experience that tells us we have sinned. Coming from that is the fear of what God will do in retaliation. We attack God; now He is going to punish us. This is the basic core of the ego system. That is where all of our guilt stems from: the belief that we have victimized God, which then we project onto all the other situations in our lives, believing we victimized other people. Very quickly that gets turned around and we believe that people victimize us.

Q: Does not the Course say that if you forgive one person, you have forgiven them all?

A: Yes. Since all difficulties stem from our guilt, if we truly forgive one person totally, we have in effect forgiven all people, because ultimately it is all the one problem.

Q: It is like hitting the headpin in bowling; all the other pins then fall down.

A: Right; that is a good analogy. There is a lovely workbook lesson that says, "I will be still an instant and go home" (workbook, p. 331; W-pI.182), which seems to suggest that you could just kind of do it like that (snap of fingers), and you are all finished. The problem is that the amount of fear that is trapped in this system is so immense. The basic source of that fear is the fear of love or the fear of God. The ego would teach

52

if you really let go of all this fear, God will destroy you. That is what keeps us from being still an instant and going home. In principle we could do that, because it is all the same, it is all one problem. But because our fear is so immense what we really do is chop away at it, so *A Course in Miracles* gets us through the chopping a little more quickly.

Q: And the fear is unconscious all the time?

A: It is unconscious because repression is the only way we could tolerate this amount of fear.

Q: I get the impression every once in a while that this is not as serious as everyone seems to think it is; some level of me always says, "Do not take this so seriously!"

A: That is absolutely right. There is a line in the Course which speaks of the separation as that time when the Son of God remembered not to laugh (text, p. 544; T-27.VIII.6:2). But that is exactly the problem. The separation was the time when the Son of God remembered not to laugh. The whole problem was that when we separated from God we took it seriously. If we had just giggled at it and realized how silly it was to try to create like God, usurping His role as Creator, none of this would have happened. What we do is make up problems, and then we take them very seriously. Then we spend the rest of our lives trying to solve the problem that is not there. It is like the Wizard of Oz; he is nothing but a little man in back of a huge amplifying system. That is what the ego is. In other places, the Course talks about how the ego seems to be a roaring lion, but is really a frightened mouse that roars at the universe (text, pp. 431, 446; T-21.VII.3:11; T-22.V.4:3). If we could learn not to take our egos so seriously, we would be much better off. What you have to watch out for, however, is that you do not deny a problem that you have made real. That is the trick, because we are very easily deluded into believing that we have let go of a problem when all we have done is cover it over.

Q: How do you know?

A: If you are doing it right, eventually you feel better, more peaceful. Earlier, we talked about the idea that "miracles are both beginnings and endings, so they alter the temporal order." This can be understood to mean that they isolate problems and say, "This is where you focus," and working that through shifts the temporal order. What you really do, since all of our problems are rooted in the past, is to say the problem is not in the past. It is really right now in the present, right here at the moment I am choosing, and I could now choose differently. Then they become the "affirmations of rebirth, which seem to go back, but really go forward." This is what the Course would mean by "to be born again," the phrase that it uses later on (e.g., text, p. 234; T-13.VI.3:5). This does not mean being born again in the way the fundamentalist Christians mean it. It means born again in the sense of choosing to live following the Holy Spirit rather than the ego. Following the ego leads to death; following the Holy Spirit leads us back to eternal life.

The miracle, really, is the affirmation of that eternal life, which then becomes being reborn in terms of our thinking differently. It seems to go back because it heals the past. If I am angry at you right at this moment, it is because I am not living with you right in this moment; I am bringing something from the past. The section later in the text that is called "Shadows of the Past" (text, p. 330; T-17.III) explains how we always see people in terms of the past, whether it be things that we believe they have done to us or to other people, or based upon our past and the kind of needs that we believed we had. So, the miracle undoes the past in the present, and that releases the future.

Therefore, the miracle takes the ego's view of time and frees us from it. The ego's view of time, which again is linear, takes the guilt of the past and projects it into the future. Because of my guilty past, I now become afraid of what the future will bring. I will feel insecure about having enough money when I am older, or I will feel insecure or fearful that something terrible is going to happen to me. All of these fears are rooted in the guilt that is in the past, which ultimately is rooted in the belief that I have sinned against God.

What the ego does in its use of time is to use the past, project it into the future, and thereby totally ignore the present.

There is a section at the beginning of Chapter 15 called "The Two Uses of Time" (text, p. 280; T-15.I) that is a very nice statement of how the ego uses time and then how the Holy Spirit does. What the Holy Spirit does is tell us that the past is nonexistent, because it is predicated on guilt that is not real. Therefore, there is nothing we have to fear in the future. Then it teaches us that the only time that is, is now; the present is the only time there is, a statement that the Course makes later (workbook, pp. 13, 236; W-pI.8.1:5; W-pI.132.3:1). That then allows the Holy Spirit to extend through us and, thus, the future becomes an extension of the present so that the peace, love, and unity we feel now become extended through us. That is what determines everything else.

Q: Would all this mean that you have to stay in a relationship?

A: No, of course not. That has to do with form or behavior, and there is nothing in *A Course in Miracles* that would ever suggest what you should do in any given situation. It simply provides the means—forgiveness—whereby you can get your ego out of the way so you can be guided by the One Who does know what is best for you in that situation. Ask the Holy Spirit first, before you do anything; but before you ask "What should I do," you should first ask His help in removing your ego investments in the outcome—one way or the other—that would interfere with your hearing His answer.

Principle 14

Miracles bear witness to truth. They are convincing because they arise from conviction. Without conviction they deteriorate into magic, which is mindless and therefore destructive; or rather, the uncreative use of mind.

Very often the Course will say things like, "bearing witness to the truth" or "reflecting truth," and what this is saying, again, is that truth is not present in this world, because there is no world. What we can do in this world is reflect the truth of

Heaven. There is a section called "The Reflection of Holiness" (text, p. 270; T-14.IX). We are not holy in this world but in Heaven. Our holiness is as Christ. What we can become in this world is the reflection of His Holiness.

There is another section with a lovely title: "Heralds of Eternity" (text, p. 404; T-20.V). The herald of eternity is the holy relationship. That is a relationship that had been unholy or special, that had been filled with guilt and anger and resentment, and now becomes healed, which means it now reflects the peace of Heaven or of eternity. The holy relationship is the forerunner of eternity. It is not eternity, but in its joining through forgiveness it reflects the oneness of Christ in Heaven. Similarly, healing reflects the perfection of Christ, the truth of who we really are. This miracle principle is saying the same thing, that miracles bear witness to the truth. They are not the truth, but they reflect the truth.

Q: The Course says that in this world of separation there is one appointed to you to be your savior, and that when you are ready to look on the face of Christ you will find that one. Does that mean that it could be anyone? Any kind of a relationship, not necessarily a male-female marriage?

A: *A Course in Miracles* seems to suggest that there are certain very, very crucial relationships in our lives, and I think that almost always these would be people that we spend a large portion of our time with: parents, children, spouses, very close friends. It could be an intense situation at work but, typically, these relationships would be what the manual says are level three relationships: life-long relationships (manual, p. 7; M-3. 5:1). They do not always have to be, but that is usually the case, and that is what the Course really is implying.

Returning to Principle 14, the miracles are convincing of this truth because they arise from the conviction that comes from within us, which really is "faith." It is the faith and the trust that by choosing the Holy Spirit's way we will be better off, which is easier said than done because we are all convinced that we know best—that anger works, separate interests work, and that our ways of solving problems are the better ones.

What makes miracles the convincing witnesses of the truth that they can become for us is to believe in them. This means to believe in the principle that by turning the problem over to the Holy Spirit, the situation will work out better.

"Without conviction, they deteriorate into magic, which is mindless and therefore destructive; or rather, the uncreative use of mind." This means that when we do not rely on the Holy Spirit, then we rely on the ego to solve the problems, and that is magic. We can define magic as anything that we do to solve a problem that is not there, which means anything we do to solve a problem on the physical level. This is how the ego would always have us solve a problem. That is magic, which may work on the level on which it occurs. If you have a splitting headache and you take an aspirin, that could take away the pain of the headache, but it will not take away the pain of the guilt that led to the headache. That is why the Course says that you should use magic if you believe in it, but do not believe that it takes care of your problems.

The miracle will show you where the problem really is. Later on, the text says that the miracle restores to cause the function of causation (text, p. 552; T-28.II.9:3), which means that miracles teach us that the cause of all our problems is in our mind. The world teaches us that the cause of all our problems is in our body, or someone else's body. For example, the reason I am not happy is that there is something wrong with me, or there is something wrong with how you treated me, or with the way the government treats me, or with the way the weather treats me, or God treats me, or the stock market treats me, or whatever else the ego makes the cause. The ego cancels out the cause in our mind, and it makes the world into the cause.

The miracle restores to cause, which is the mind, the function of causation. Basically, all the miracle does is say the problem is not in someone else; it is in me. What magic says is that the problem is in the world or the body, and so that is where you have to solve the problem. We are all very ingenious at solving the world's problems, and medicine is getting better and better at solving the body's problems. But it does not truly solve any problem, because all the ego does is make up another one. In this generation, cancer is the thing. It used to be polio, I remember. And then, for the next generation it will be something else. We just keep changing the forms and never get to the real cause of the problem, which is our belief in separation.

When we use magic as a way to solve problems in the world, it can be "destructive." (By the way, the use of this word is another example of what frequently happened in the early weeks of the dictation of the Course, an example of its conversational nature. Helen's hearing of the word "destructive" was immediately corrected to "uncreative use of mind.") That is because the world's way of solving problems is through attack. Sometimes the attack is very subtle; other times it obviously is not subtle. But magic is never loving because it is always an attempt to solve a problem through being unloving, which excludes the Source of love in our mind.

Principle 15

Each day should be devoted to miracles. The purpose of time is to enable you to learn how to use time constructively. It is thus a teaching device and a means to an end. Time will cease when it is no longer useful in facilitating learning.

Basically, this principle is talking about the fundamental goal of the Course, which is to help us spend every hour of our day, all the days of our lives, continually seeing things as the Holy Spirit has us see them. This means to continue to see everything that occurs in our lives as a lesson that He would have us learn—that every single thing that occurs is a learning opportunity if we avail ourselves of that learning. Thus, everything that confronts us should be seen as an opportunity of choosing either the ego's grievance or the Holy Spirit's miracle.

Q: There are times during the day when my ego screams so loud that I do not remember to turn to the Holy Spirit. If I began my day with a blanket statement: "Holy Spirit, please be with me all day," would that happen?

A: I doubt it. If you do that and then do not think of Him at any other point, that is magic. What *A Course in Miracles* would say is that you should start your day that way and think of Him all the rest of the day, too. Otherwise, you are going to hope that going on automatic pilot will take care of everything. In one sense that is true, if you really go on automatic pilot. But I think that that requires a tremendous amount of discipline, and if we had that kind of discipline, then we would not need a workbook. In the beginning of Chapter 30 is a section called "Rules for Decision" (text, p. 581; T-30.I) which actually is a very simple way of telling us how we should begin. It says exactly what you are saying, but then it elaborates on what you should do when you forget. I think that we should start our day like that, but then we should continually reinforce it. Otherwise, it is very, very easy to fall back onto the ego.

Q: I find one of the reasons why I cannot always remember to ask to see it through the vision of the Holy Spirit is that there is a part of me, in spite of all my conscious decisions, that still wants to see it my way. Now, that is not a conscious part of me. It is always a shock when I discover it is there. What do you do about the unconscious?

A: When you do become aware of it, you do not feel guilty about it, and what you try to do is become more and more sensitive to when that unconscious part manifests itself. That is what happens when you work with this material a while. It may seem as if your life is getting worse or you are becoming more unhappy. What is really happening is that you are becoming more sensitive to things in yourself that otherwise you would not have known about. What you try to do is just be aware of when you are projecting. It is a lot of hard work, and it is not easy. It requires a vigilance.

The third lesson of the Holy Spirit in Chapter 6, "Be Vigilant Only for God and His Kingdom" (text, p. 100; T-6.V.C), really means be vigilant against the ego; and it does require a lot of hard work. This really is mind training, always to be thinking of the other way of looking at something. There is a line in the text that drives everyone crazy because everyone recognizes what it means. It says, "Do you prefer that you be right or happy?" (text, p. 573; T-29.VII.1:9).

Q: Just on the same topic, there is a section in the Course that deals with a set of questions, and the last one answers the three before it; it asks the question . . .

A: "And do I want to see what I denied *because* it is the truth?" (text, p. 432; T-21.VII.5:14) All this is really part of that last obstacle to peace, the fear of God (text, p. 391; T-19.IV.D), because the ego is always teaching us that the truth, if we were really to look at it, would destroy us. The truth of us is so awful and so devastating, because we are such wretched people, that if we really looked at it, God would strike us dead. What has to happen is that we chip away at the thought system which teaches us that and realize the truth is not that we are this terrible person, but that we are this holy person who is God's Son. That takes a lot of work because the other thought system is so much a part of us.

The section called "The Fear to Look Within" (text, p. 423; T-21.IV) first describes what the ego tells us we would see if we looked within: a hopelessly sinful person. Then it says, but what if you looked within and you saw that there was no sin? That is the real fear; but it is the ego's fear. That is why we prefer to look at things our way rather than God's way. If the world is an hallucination and we made it all up, and, furthermore, this world was made as an attack on God, as the Course teaches (workbook, p. 403; W-pII.3.2:1), then it means that this world is a great symbol of our sin against God. If it is not there, then the whole thing is made up; it is just all silly fluff. This is when the ego gets terrified. That the whole world of sin is nothing but just a silly mistake is the one thing the ego will never let us look at. That is why, when the Course repeatedly says there is no sin, the ego does not like that at all. The entire ego thought system is predicated on sin. That is what makes this world real, which means it denies the reality of God's Will.

"The purpose of time is to enable you to learn how to use time constructively." That is what I said earlier: The purpose of time is to teach us that there is no time. It is, thus, a teaching device and a means to an end, which is the way *A Course in Miracles* looks at everything in this world. Nothing in the world is an end in itself; nothing is real in itself; it is merely a teaching device. But do not deny the world or the body; that is not what the Course teaches. Rather, we should look at them differently. Everything that occurs, to the extent that it pushes our buttons or upsets us in any way, becomes an opportunity for us to learn our lessons. This not only includes things in our personal world, but in the larger world as well—things like famine, the Holocaust, the crucifixion. We do not deny them or their occurrence within the world of illusion, but we do change the way we look at them: from victims and victimizers, to all people—including ourselves—calling out for the love we do not believe we deserve.

This whole world is a classroom: our individual lives are individual classes that we take within this university. This whole path then becomes like a curriculum that we have to learn, and our individual experiences become specific classes that we take to undo the guilt that we have made specific. That is the purpose of the world, the purpose of time.

"Time will cease when it is no longer useful in facilitating learning." When we have fulfilled the purpose of time, when every last separated child of God returns to his or her right mind—that is what *A Course in Miracles* calls the Second Coming, which is the awakening of the Son from his bad dream. This makes way for the Last Judgment, which is the final sorting out of truth from illusion. That is when the entire world disappears, as the Course says, back into the nothingness from which it came (manual, p. 81; C-4.4:5).

Principle 16

Miracles are teaching devices for demonstrating it is as blessed to give as to receive. They simultaneously increase the strength of the giver and supply strength to the receiver.

This is the same idea as Principle 9. You can see that a lot of the principles now are going to repeat themselves. Just as with time, the miracle is a teaching device, and the idea is to help us realize that we are not separate.

The miracle teaches us that "to give and to receive are one in truth," which by the way, is the title of workbook lesson 108. We are all the same: teacher and pupil; therapist and patient; the one who heals and the one who is healed. Remember that the error that the miracle has to correct is the error of believing we are separate. The miracle, then, becomes an expression of our joining, and that is what this principle is talking about.

Principle 17

Miracles transcend the body. They are sudden shifts into invisibility, away from the bodily level. That is why they heal.

"Miracles transcend the body" because they teach us the body is not where "it's at." The body is not what the problem is and, therefore, by changing our minds we can transcend the laws of the body. That is why for example, people who may have serious problems with cancer, one day go to the doctor who says, "I do not understand it; everything is all cleared up." There are lots of different examples of that kind of process.

There is a lesson that says, "I am under no laws but God's" (workbook, p. 132; W-pI.76). That lesson mentions some of the laws that the world holds dear, such as the laws of nutrition, immunization, friendship, economics, and religion, and says that none of these laws means anything at all, and by shifting to the miracle (right-mindedness), one can transcend these laws and not be bound by them. It was the mind that made up the physical laws. That is why it is so important to realize, if you are going to work with *A Course in Miracles*, that it teaches that God did not create this world. The laws of this world, the laws of gravity, death, sickness, and nutrition—all the laws— are "man-made"; they are all part of the ego mind. The ego made them, and we give those laws power by virtue of our allegiance to the ego. By shifting that allegiance, we could then transcend all those laws.

There are certain people such as Sai Baba, the famous Indian guru, who transcends the physical world by manifesting and materializing things in his hand. He will just wave his hand and, all of a sudden, come out with a diamond ring or whatever it is he wants to do. And one does not have to believe, by the way, that he is authentic to accept that the principle is authentic. That is really what he is demonstrating: that by proper use of your mind you can actually do anything in this world. As Jesus says later on in the text, your faith can move mountains (text, p. 421; T-21.III.3:1), and I think he means that very literally. Since our minds made up the mountain anyway, why can we not play around with it or move it around if we so choose? Since everything is made by our minds, it should not be any surprise that we can change what we have already made. What is the big deal? We made cancer; why can we not change our minds about it? It is not the Holy Spirit who heals cancer. He merely reminds us that we can make another choice, appealing to the power of our mind to change itself. The forms are magic, but the purpose with Sai Baba certainly appears to be the demonstration, to minds that are closed to their power, of what the mind can do. And it is this purpose that makes it spiritual, not psychic, a distinction we will return to later (see pp. 74, 101).

Another example is the one that Ram Dass cites in terms of his guru. Then called Richard Alpert, the Harvard psychologist who collaborated with Timothy Leary on psychedelic research and experimentation, he traveled to India in search of his guru and finally found him. After a few days, the guru asked him to bring his suitcase, which was filled with LSD and whatever else, supposedly unknown to the guru. Alpert tried to conceal it all, but finally, upon the guru's prodding, had to hand it over to him. Without batting an eye, the guru swallowed what Alpert states was an incredible amount of the "white stuff." It had no effect on the guru whatsoever. It was an example of psychic ability or magic, but its purpose was certainly different. And it had quite an effect on Alpert.

These are illustrations of the first principle—that there is no order of difficulty. A lot of people are able to train their minds so that they can move a glass or a cup from one part of the table to another. That is not very hard to do if you really are dedicated and disciplined in your mind. And, if you can move a cup, why could you not move a mountain? This could be a way of explaining how the ancient Egyptians moved all those heavy stones to construct the pyramids: that they had somehow learned to master their minds. To deny this as a possibility is to state that there is an order of difficulty in miracles.

Such mastery, however, does not bring you peace, and it does not bring you closer to God. All that it does is enable you to get back in touch with the power of your mind. But it is the misuse of that power that got us into trouble in the first place. So, the only remedy for that misuse is to place your mind under the guidance of the One Who will never misuse it. This is why the Course is so clear and emphatic about how we are to do things in the world—we ask the One Who does know; we do not do them on our own. Otherwise, we could use our minds as a way of achieving power over other people, hurting them and ourselves.

When the principle says that the miracle "shifts into invisibility," it is talking about shifting to the mind rather than to the body. And that is why the miracle can heal, because it brings the problem back to where the problem really is, which is the mind and not the body. There is a lovely line near the end of Chapter 12 which says: "When you made visible what is not true, what *is* true became invisible to you" (text p. 217; T-12.VIII.3:1). Therefore, we need help in shifting away from what appears visible—the body—to what we have made invisible—the truth in our minds.

Principle 18

A miracle is a service. It is the maximal service you can render to another. It is a way of loving your neighbor as yourself. You recognize your own and your neighbor's worth simultaneously.

That is another way of saying what we have already talked about, that the miracle helps us recognize and remember that we are one and the same, and that our worth is established by God. Your worth is the same as mine. If I see you as being worthier than I, or less worthy than I am—victim or victimizer—then that is an attack. It is basically an attack on the Sonship and, therefore, must be an attack on the Creator of the Sonship. It is a consistent teaching of *A Course in Miracles* that we are all the same, moving beyond the superficial differences of our bodies—physical and psychological—to the underlying unity of not only the Christ in us, but also our shared need to remember what we have forgotten and to escape from the prison of our own guilt. Thus, at the end of Chapter 15, which was written around New Year's, there is this little prayer: "Make this year different by making it all the same" (text, p. 306; T-15.XI.10:11). We learn to see everything the same because there is, in truth, only one problem, and thus there can be only one solution. And all things and all people in the world but serve to teach us this one lesson.

A miracle is a service because, obviously, it is a way of bringing love to someone who believes in fear, and by bringing love or being a channel of love to you who are fearful, I am also channeling it to myself. Again, the miracle is not behavioral, despite what may sometimes appear to be behavioral effects. It is only on the level of the mind. The most loving thing we can ever do has nothing to do with what we do on the level of form. It is rather our joining with each other through forgiveness.

Principle 19

Miracles make minds one in God. They depend on cooperation because the Sonship is the sum of all that God created. Miracles therefore reflect the laws of eternity, not of time.

Basically, this means that what miracles do is restore to our mind the awareness of our oneness in God. Miracles do not *make* us one in God; miracles *remind* us that we are one in

God. Remember, once again, the key idea in the ego system and the ego's way of perceiving is that we are separate. If I believe that my body is sick, then I am making my body real, which means I am making the body's purpose real. This is separation. If I become upset because you are sick, I am doing the very same thing.

"They depend on cooperation because the Sonship is the sum of all that God created." This expresses the same idea: Cooperation means that you join with someone. And the Sonship of God is one.

The other thing the Course repeatedly says of itself, besides that it saves time, is that it is simple. By this it does not mean that it is easy. It is simple because it sees everything exactly the same way. All problems are the same; all people are the same. We are all joined on the level of our minds. Therefore, it makes the solution to all problems the same.

Q: Would that also include joining with people who have gone before us?

A: Yes, sure. Relationships are not of the body, so that you could have someone you were close to who has died, and still have a meaningful relationship with him or her.

"Miracles therefore reflect the laws of eternity, not of time." There's that word "reflect" again. The miracle does not follow the law of eternity, because eternity has nothing to do with the world of time. The miracle is only needed in the world of time. So the miracle reflects the law of eternity. The law of eternity is that we are all one, and we are all one right now.

Principle 20

Miracles reawaken the awareness that the spirit, not the body, is the altar of truth. This is the recognition that leads to the healing power of the miracle.

That is, again, the same idea, that truth and holiness are not found in the body; they are found in our minds. When our minds are totally healed we will recall that truth is in our Identity as spirit. Later on, the Course talks about the temple of the Holy Spirit as a relationship (text, p. 407; T-20.VI.5:1). It is not in the body; it is in the relationship. The Holy Spirit cannot be in the body because there is no body. God would not place the Holy Spirit in a place that does not exist and where there is no problem. Bodies do not get sick, nor do they get well. It is only the mind that can be sick, and only the mind that can be healed.

I said earlier that when the separation seemed to occur, God created the Holy Spirit. He placed the Holy Spirit, Who is also defined in the Course as being God's Answer and His Voice, in the place where He is needed (text, pp. 68f; T-5.I.5; T-5.II.2). Where the Holy Spirit is needed is not out here in the world, because the world is not the problem. He is needed in our mind. That is where the altar of truth is. The body is not the temple of the Holy Spirit; it is the *use* of the body that is, which is always found in terms of a relationship: joining in a common purpose. For the Course, the temple of the Holy Spirit, where He is made manifest and where He is found, is in a relationship. There is a passage where Jesus says that he stands within the holy relationship (text, p. 385; T-19.IV.B.5:3; 8:3). This does not mean that he is not present in an unholy relationship. What it means is that when we are in an unholy relationship, which is what *A Course in Miracles* calls a "special relationship," a relationship where guilt is the goal and separation is the principle, then the one who manifests forgiveness and joining will become invisible to us. If we are choosing to hear the ego's voice of guilt and separation, we are not going to hear the voice or experience the presence of the one who represents joining, forgiveness, and healing. It is not that Jesus is not present in a special relationship, but his presence is obscured.

When he says he stands within the holy relationship, he means that when we truly forgive and shift the purpose of the relationship from the ego's guilt to his forgiveness, then we will know he is there. The veils of guilt that kept him hidden are removed. He says in the Course at one point, "Teach not that I died in vain. Teach rather that I did not die by demonstrating that I live in you" (text, p. 193; T-11.VI.7:3–4). The way that we demonstrate that Jesus is alive and well, and that he did do what he said he did, is to live according to the same principle that he did: the principle of forgiveness or transcendence of the body; totally shifting from a perception of seeing oneself as a victim to seeing oneself as joined with all people, living that out in the relationships of our personal lives. That is how we demonstrate that he is living in us. In words based on John's gospel: "They will know you are my disciples by your love for one another" (Jn 13:35). The Course's version of that would be: "They will know you are my disciples by your forgiveness of each other."

The whole idea of the miracle, again, is to shift from the body and the focus on the body back to the mind. That is where the altar to truth is; that is where God is found. This is the recognition that leads to the healing power of the miracle. What heals, then, is realizing: 1) where the problem is; that is, it is not in our body but it is in our mind; and 2) realizing Who is the One Who will heal this mind. Thus, we should not be focusing on behavior, what is outside us, for that is not the criterion of good or bad, sickness or health. As Hamlet says: "There is nothing either good or bad, but thinking makes it so" (II,ii). It is our thoughts that are important (the content); not our actions (the form).

Principle 21

Miracles are natural signs of forgiveness. Through miracles you accept God's forgiveness by extending it to others.

Here is the first statement in the Course on forgiveness. As I mentioned right at the beginning, God does not forgive. When *A Course in Miracles* talks about the forgiveness of God, it really is talking about the Love of God.

Q: I thought that miracles were forgiveness.

A: They are. That is why I have said it is all the same thing:

"miracle," "forgiveness," "healing," "Atonement." They are just different words to describe the same process. You could actually give a whole list of words that all say the same kind of thing: "vision," "the real world," "the holy instant," "the holy relationship," "salvation," "redemption," "correction," "the face of Christ," "Christ's vision," "true perception." They are different words that reflect different aspects of the same basic process.

Basically, forgiveness, as the Course defines it elsewhere, is forgiving your brother for what he has not done. In other words, you realize that nothing has been done to you; it is all something that you did to yourself. What happens with miracles is that we shift from the ego's attack and hatred to the Holy Spirit's Love, which then becomes the extension of God's Love to us, and then through us to other people. This is what the Course means by forgiveness. It is an example of the passage I just quoted where Jesus says that we demonstrate that he did not die in vain by demonstrating that he lives in us, which means that we live according to the same principles of forgiveness that he demonstrated. And the more we do what he says, the more we will understand what he taught and the closer we will come to him. Similarly with the Course, the more we can practice its lessons of undoing guilt through forgiveness, the more we will be able to understand what the text is saying. And of course the more we can understand it, the easier it becomes to apply in our daily lives. It is a reciprocal process.

Principle 22

Miracles are associated with fear only because of the belief that darkness can hide. You believe that what your physical eyes cannot see does not exist. This leads to a denial of spiritual sight.

Let me spend a little time on this one. The ego teaches us that the core of our being is this dark sinful spot which is our guilt, and that this is who we really are. There is a workbook lesson that says that if you really looked within, you would believe that if people saw you the way you believe you are, they would recoil as if jumping back from a poisonous snake (workbook, p. 159; W-pI.93.1:1–2). We feel that we are wretched, sinful persons. Then we believe that somehow we could be protected from the horror of ever getting too close to this by defending ourselves with all the things the ego uses. These are what Freud called the mechanisms of defense, and most important of these are denial and projection. We make believe this is not what we are, after we first made believe that it is exactly what we are. Then we try to hide from it by putting a cloak of unconsciousness around it and projecting it out. Finally, I no longer see that dark spot of guilt in me; I see it in others and I attack them for it.

This means that we believe that this defense can hide what is underneath. By projecting onto someone else, I believe that my guilt can be hidden from me. This is the belief that darkness can hide. The "darkness" in this statement can be equated with the word "defense." My defense can hide this, which means that I need my defense to protect me from my own guilt. The ego teaches me that if I give this up, I am going to have nothing to protect me from my guilt, and I am going to be in a lot of trouble. The ego teaches that defenses protect us; darkness can hide. This, then, builds up the fear that if I give the darkness up, I am going to be thoroughly exposed to this guilt and I will be in trouble. The ego never tells us that defenses do not hide: the fact that I do not see the guilt does not mean it is not there.

An important line that occurs later on in the text says that "defenses *do* what they would defend" (text, p. 334; T-17.IV.7:1), which is a very important principle. The reason that we invest such time and effort and energy into maintaining defenses is that we believe they will protect us from what we are afraid of. The purpose of all our defenses is to defend us against our guilt. What the ego never tells us is that the more that we invest in a defense, the more we are saying there is, indeed, something horrible inside us. If I did not have this horrible guilt, then I would not have to bother with the defense. Therefore, the more that I invest in having a defense against my guilt, which I am afraid of, the more fearful I am going to get because the fact that I have the defense is telling me, "You had better watch it; there is something inside of you that is vulnerable." That is what *A Course in Miracles* means when it says that "defenses *do* what they would defend." Their purpose is to protect us from fear, but they really reinforce the fear. The ego never tells us that.

In a very powerful section in Chapter 27 of the text called "The Fear of Healing" (text, p. 528; T-27.II), the Course makes it clear why the ego teaches us to be afraid of the miracle and healing. The ego teaches that if you choose the miracle and give up the defenses of attack (i.e., see your brother as your friend and not your enemy), you will have no place to project your guilt. It will then remain with you and destroy you. And then the fear really grows.

That is another example of what the Course means a little later on when it says that when you begin to hear the Holy Spirit's Voice and pay attention to what He says, your ego will become vicious (text, p. 164; T-9.VII.4:4–7). The ego's viciousness is always some expression of fear, of terror, which then gets projected into anger, disruptiveness, etc. The ego teaches us that if we let go of our defenses, then all hell will break loose, literally. Psychologists fall into the same trap when they teach that if you do not have defenses you will go psychotic. It is really the opposite. If you do not have defenses you will go sane; you will not go psychotic. But that does not mean that you strip people's defenses away. The process has to be very gentle and loving, and the therapist often has to be very patient. To repeat, this does not mean that we should strip all the defenses away. What it does mean is that if you follow the Holy Spirit's guidance, the goal will be to have no defenses. And then when you look within, you will not see sin; you will see that there was no sin. That is the end of the journey.

"Miracles are associated with fear only because of the belief that darkness can hide." Once you can recognize that darkness cannot hide, that defenses do not do what they say that they do, then you are ready to take the next step, which is explained later on in Chapter 1 of the text. Then you realize that there is nothing that has to be hidden because this guilt is not anything terrible; it is just a silly belief system that will disappear. This is why we are afraid of choosing a miracle, which translates to why we are afraid to truly forgive someone, to really let go of the past and realize that we are not victims, no matter how convincingly the experiences of the world would teach us that belief. We all are very good at rationalizing why we do not want to give all of this up. The real reason we do not want to give it up is that we do not want to be peaceful. That is what the Course talks about later as the ego's attraction of guilt (text, p. 382; T-19.IV.A.i). We would rather be guilty and make guilt real; then we have to defend against it.

We believe that what our physical eyes cannot see does not exist. This is really the principle of the ostrich, which is the principle of repression or denial. If I do not see a problem, it does not exist. If I cover over my guilt, then it is not there. That is the idea again that darkness can hide. This then leads to a denial of "spiritual sight," the term the early sections of the Course use for "vision." And, when *A Course in Miracles* talks about vision, or spiritual sight, it is not talking about seeing with one's eyes. It is talking about seeing with the Holy Spirit's eyes, which is an attitude. It has nothing to do with physical sight.

Principle 23

Miracles rearrange perception and place all levels in true perspective. This is healing because sickness comes from confusing the levels.

The levels that are being confused are the levels of the mind and the body. The ego takes the problem of guilt in our minds, which is the true sickness, and it says it is not the mind that is sick, it is the body that is sick. It shifts from the level of the mind back to the level of the body. The miracle takes it right back to where it started and says it is not the body that is sick, it is the mind that is sick.

That is all the miracle does. It brings the problem back to where it is. Again, it restores to cause (the mind) the function of causation. The Course is very, very emphatic on that. There is nothing whatsoever that is sick with the body. The body does nothing at all. It is totally neutral. There is a workbook lesson that says, "My body is a wholly neutral thing" (workbook, p. 435; W-pII.294). The body merely carries out the dictates of the mind. As I said just before, the body cannot be healed because the body has never been sick. It is the mind that is sick and, therefore, it is the mind that has to be healed. The sickness of the mind is separation, or guilt; the healing of the mind is forgiveness, or joining. The miracle brings that about by shifting the problem back to where it is.

Principle 24

Miracles enable you to heal the sick and raise the dead because you made sickness and death yourself, and can therefore abolish both. *You* **are a miracle, capable of creating in the likeness of your Creator. Everything else is your own nightmare, and does not exist. Only the creations of light are real.**

One of the signs that the Bible says people used, to know that Jesus was the Messiah, was that he healed the sick and raised the dead. But, obviously, the Bible does not teach that we made sickness and death ourselves. This is what we talked about earlier. The mind made up everything in this world. *A Course in Miracles* really means this in the all-inclusive cosmic sense of making up the entire physical universe. For our purposes here, it is saying that we made the body and the body's laws, which means we made the laws of sickness and we made the laws of death. Because we did that, we can change them.

The Holy Spirit does not heal the sick body because He did not make the body sick. What the Holy Spirit does is heal the guilt in our minds that made the body sick by helping us change our minds about the guilt we chose. This is a very important distinction to keep in mind, so you do not fall into the trap of asking the Holy Spirit's help for something in the material world. All that does, again, is make the world real, just as you should not ask the Holy Spirit for a parking space. That is a favorite one with people who work with the Course.

Q: But when you use your mind to project things like that, that is not necessarily calling on the Holy Spirit. That is using your mind.

A: There is a difference between the psychic and the spiritual. The psychic is something that we do with *our* minds; the spiritual is something we do with *His* mind. There is a big difference between the two. And we can get very impressed with the psychic things that we are all capable of. Finding parking spots may be one of them. But to attribute that to the Holy Spirit is a mistake, because He does not do things in the world; He does things in our minds. There is no world. To believe the Holy Spirit operates in the world is to make Him as insane as we are: seeing a problem where there is no problem. The problem is not that you need a parking space; the problem is your *concern* about needing the parking space.

You are telling Him that you need a parking spot. The better prayer would be to ask His help to relieve you of any concern that you find a parking spot. How do you know where you are supposed to park? Maybe you are supposed to park three blocks away from where you think you are supposed to park, because of reasons you do not know about. Maybe you are supposed to park three blocks away, because on your walk from where your car is parked to where you are supposed to go, you are going to meet someone you are supposed to meet, that you otherwise would never know about. In other words, it is a very subtle way of trying to control Him and tell Him what you need, and often we will ask His help in those things that we think we are saving time on, but maybe we would save time even more by making that three-block walk and having certain experiences which would enable us to save time on our Atonement path.

Q: I am getting a double message here. On one hand, I am hearing you say that it does not make any difference if you project a parking space or what you do as long as you do not attribute that to the Holy Spirit. But now you are saying the opposite, which is do not project parking spaces or any such thing, they are all in the mind.

A: Right, I am saying both things. I am saying that the best thing is not to use magic at all, but most of us are not up to that all the time. The best thing would be to ask the Holy Spirit, "What should I do?" rather than to project the parking spot. What I am saying is that there is nothing wrong in doing that, except that I do not think it will save you the time that asking the Holy Spirit will, in terms of saving you time in working through your own guilt.

Later on, the Course talks about how the Holy Spirit perceives totally, which would be another way of saying He perceives the whole situation. We usually perceive a specific thing, a specific need at some point. I do not want to walk ten blocks or ten minutes or this or that. I want to get to this appointment on time; I do not want to be stuck in traffic. We just see it within a very narrow band in our experience. He sees it in a much larger plan, and that is why the more open we can be, the more quickly we can learn His lessons and be healed.

Q: When I first started using the Course I used to ask the Holy Spirit for a myriad of things, and now my feeling is His only function really is to teach me forgiveness. I do not even ask for things any more; I just keep asking Him to help me be less resistant about being a forgiving and loving person. That is really the only way I see the Holy Spirit's function. I do not think He is here to tell me where I should be and what I should do. I do not know if I am wrong or right, but...

A: That is the whole idea. What you pray for, if you find yourself in a specific situation that is giving you anxiety, is for help in not being anxious, rather than praying for help that the situation be resolved in the way that you need it to be.

Q: In light of what you said about sickness, I wonder how you get sick. What brings us back to being healthy again?

A: You get sick by projecting the guilt in your mind onto your body, and forgiveness brings you back to health. If you get a cold, then what you should do, after you take aspirins or cold pills or whatever else, is ask for help in forgiving whomever it is you have not forgiven. If no one comes to mind, just start wherever you are.

Q: But we know that because we are here listening to you. How about those who do not know that? How do they get well?

A: Either by changing their minds through forgiveness or by using some form of magic. Magic works; there is no question about that. But that is not going to relieve the underlying cause of the cold, or whatever the sickness is. Most people in the world go through solving problems on this level, one problem after another. As I said earlier, we are getting more and more sophisticated at solving our problems, which means the ego is becoming more and more sophisticated in making problems up. And it never ends. The only thing that ends the whole cycle is to forgive. That is why we are still fighting the same wars today that we were fighting centuries and millennia ago.

Q: So you are saying then to concentrate on the cause not the effect.

A: Right. The cause would always be some aspect of guilt.

"*You* are a miracle, capable of creating in the likeness of your Creator." Obviously, when it says *you* are a miracle, "miracle" is used in a much different context from how we are talking about it. We are capable of creating in the likeness of our Creator. That is what creation is. We extend our spiritual Self, as Christ, just as God extended His spiritual Self in creating us. Remember, creation is not possible in this world.

"Everything else is your own nightmare, and does not exist. Only the creations of light are real." That is a very clear statement of the Level One distinction between truth and illusion. Creating in the likeness of God, which is on the level of spirit, is the only truth; nothing else exists in this world. It seems to, but everything else is nothing but a bad dream. At the moment we separated from God, we fell asleep. Everything that followed from that, this whole carpet of time, this whole world of evolution, is nothing more than a bad dream.

Let me mention, because it does not come up in these principles, that the goal of *A Course in Miracles* is not to awaken from the dream. The goal is to change the nightmare dream into a happy dream. In the happy dream, we are still living within this world of illusion, the world of separate bodies, but no longer projecting any guilt onto it. It is living in this world with what is called "true perception." That is what the Course terms "the real world": it is a world totally without sin in our minds. That is the goal of the Course. Then it says that God takes the last step Himself, and that is what finally awakens us from the dream entirely. But the focus of *A Course in Miracles* is to help us live in this world, which is a world of the body, but without the projections of guilt.

Principle 25

Miracles are part of an interlocking chain of forgiveness which, when completed, is the Atonement. Atonement works all the time and in all the dimensions of time.

This is the first statement of the Atonement. Let me just say a couple of words about what the Atonement is, as the Course uses the word. Please do not read the word as "at-one-ment." That is a common New Age word, and many people come to *A Course in Miracles* and read it that way. First, it is not what the Course means; and second, it takes away from one of the Course's purposes, that of using Christian language and terminology in a different way. If you change the word to "at-one-ment," you are going to lose that meaning.

The word "Atonement" is basically a synonym for the word "correction," and is the Course's term for the overall plan that came into existence with the Holy Spirit to undo the error of believing we are separate. The Holy Spirit was placed in our mind by God, and reunites us with the Father we thought we left. The Holy Spirit is the connecting link between ourselves and God, which thereby undoes the separation, correcting the error. So, we could say that the Holy Spirit really is the expression of the Atonement principle, which is that the separation from God never truly happened. The word "Atonement" is the Course word for the overall plan of awakening the Son of God from his nightmare that he was separate.

The word is also used in a narrower sense to describe the individual Atonement plan that each of us has to complete. The Course says that our only responsibility is to accept the Atonement for ourselves (text, p. 22; T-2.V.5:1). That means that we must accept the denial of the reality of the separation, and the unreality of guilt in the specific relationships and situations that we confront. Atonement, then, has meaning on an individual level, which is our own particular path. In other words, this carpet of time is made up of thousands and millions of little threads, and each thread represents the individual life we call our own. Each of us must undo the beliefs that go into each thread, and that is the Atonement. When every last child of God completes his or her plan, the overall plan of Atonement is complete. That is how the word is used.

It has specific meaning in the context of the Course in terms of the purpose I mentioned before, that Christianity has taught that Atonement only comes through sacrifice and suffering. There is a very powerful section at the beginning of Chapter 3 called "Atonement Without Sacrifice" (text, p. 32; T-3.I), which specifically deals with the crucifixion of Jesus and talks about how its purpose was not to atone for sin by suffering, sacrifice, and death. That is a belief that comes from people's guilt. The true Atonement is to correct that misbelief by recognizing that the body is not real, that sin is not real, and that it is all a bad dream. Again, the word "Atonement" is synonymous with correction.

Basically, through choosing the miracle we are really choosing to forgive, and the more we do that, the more we are able to extend this forgiveness to other people. When that whole process or chain is completed, that is the Atonement. This is an image the Course uses in other places. It talks about how a strong chain of Atonement is welded each time we choose a miracle (text, p. 8; T-1.III.9:2). There is a section called "The

Circle of Atonement" (text, p. 262; T-14.V) which has the same idea. It is an ever-widening circle; we draw more and more people into the plan of the Atonement through our forgiveness of them.

"Atonement works all the time and in all the dimensions of time." The phrase, "all the dimensions of time," reflects the idea of a hologram, which I mentioned earlier (see p. 49). It can be understood in terms of another statement which says that behind each brother stand a thousand more (text, p. 537; T-27.V.10:4). In forgiving you, I am also forgiving all the other people in my life, or other lives, who have represented the same problem. All minds are joined. If I have a problem, let us say an authority problem, then behind you as a specific example of that, would be all the other people in my life with whom I have had the same problem. So that Atonement corrects and heals all aspects of the same issue, even when we are not aware of it. Again, "Atonement" refers to the individual level as well as to the collective one.

Principle 26

Miracles represent freedom from fear. "Atoning" means "undoing." The undoing of fear is an essential part of the Atonement value of miracles.

To look with the ego's eyes really is the same as to look with the eyes of fear. We would never try to attack or hurt others if we were not afraid of them. By choosing the Holy Spirit instead of the ego, we are really choosing love instead of fear.

"Atoning" means "undoing," which is another word for "correction." Basically, when we atone for our sin, we undo the belief in it. We do not make it real and then try to undo it, which of course is the way the world—the theological, psychological worlds, etc.—usually proceeds. There are two sections, "The Unreality of Sin" (text, p. 376; T-19.III) and "Sin versus Error" (text, p. 374; T-19.II), that point out that you deny the reality of sin by changing it to a mistake. As the Course teaches: Sins are punished, mistakes are corrected.

This does not mean that you deny what you see. You do not deny what you read about in the newspapers or what people have done. What you do is shift your interpretation from sin, which is always a projection of our own belief in sin, to a mistake that has to be corrected, which is our own as well as the other person's. Once again, sins are punished by the ego; mistakes are corrected by the Holy Spirit. And, thus, they are undone.

Principle 27

A miracle is a universal blessing from God through me to all my brothers. It is the privilege of the forgiven to forgive.

This is the first time that the person of Jesus appears in the Course. The miracle has its source in God and is expressed through Jesus. Jesus, being the manifestation of the Holy Spirit, thus brings the Love of God through us to other people, bridging the gulf between ourselves and God. That is what a miracle does. And as we forgive, we are forgiven, which really means we accept God's Love. Of course, the more we accept forgiveness, the more we would want to forgive other people. It is a reciprocal process. It is always important to remember that Jesus does the miracles, not us. Our job is only to clear our minds of what would interfere so that he can extend his love through us.

Principle 28

Miracles are a way of earning release from fear. Revelation induces a state in which fear has already been abolished. Miracles are thus a means and revelation is an end.

Obviously, it does not mean "earning"; it is really a way of achieving release from fear. A distinction is being made between revelation and miracle. When we have a revelation, in that instant there is absolutely no fear in us whatsoever. Something in us has made a total shift, and we are totally open to God. That does not last, however. If it did, we would not be here. Revelations are temporary, and then we will revert to whatever ego issues are still present.

Q: Are those like holy instants?

A: Well, it would be like a full holy instant.

Principle 29

Miracles praise God through you. They praise Him by honoring His creations, affirming their perfection. They heal because they deny body-identification and affirm spirit-identification.

One of the Judaeo-Christian ideas is that we should praise God. Certainly a lot of the Psalms have that aspect to them. Clearly, though, God does not need us to praise Him. He does not have an ego that would require people to praise Him (text, p. 64; T-4.VII.6:1–3). The way in which a miracle praises God is by simply reflecting His being and His all-inclusive Love, not by words or actions.

One way special love is distinguished from real love is that special love is always an exclusive phenomenon. It always excludes certain people. The Love of God is all-inclusive; He makes no exceptions. As the Bible says, God has no favorites. Miracles praise this Love of God by uniting all people in our mind. "They praise Him by honoring His creations, affirming their perfection." The miracle is a shift from seeing someone as imperfect, whether we see that person as an imperfect body because he or she is physically sick, or we see that person as imperfect because we have judged him or her as being sinful. We then shift from that perception to the Holy Spirit's perception which looks beyond the error to the truth, looks beyond the darkness of the ego to the light of Christ that shines in that person.

"They heal because they deny body-identification and affirm spirit-identification." This idea is the same as that expressed in Principle 17. They heal because they move away from identifying with the body, which is not the problem, by identifying with the spirit. It is the spirit that is the source of the answer. And by identifying with Who we really are, we are recognizing that everything else is merely a defense against this truth.

Q: Can you do that and not recognize where they are mentally or physically? In other words, denying what you are seeing, and wanting to see the perfection of the person.

A: There is a way of looking that the Course sets forth, which is like a double vision. You do not deny what your eyes see; you do not deny someone who is in physical pain or someone who has some need or whatever. But at the same time, you are also realizing that what you are seeing is a call for help. That is what *A Course in Miracles* calls the judgment of the Holy Spirit (text, p. 200; T-12.I): that the sickness and the pain, or the anger and the attack, whatever it is the person has done, is really a call for help and an expression of that person's identification with his or her ego.

Q: In a specific instance, how far do I take it?

A: You say to the Holy Spirit or to Jesus or whomever you feel you are talking to: "What would you have me do?" If you find yourself getting upset by the person's problem, whatever the level is, then before you ask Him what you should do, you should ask His help that your perception be healed. That is what is meant by "the only meaningful prayer is for forgiveness" (text, p. 40; T-3.V.6:3). You first ask that He help you shift from the ego's way of looking to His way of looking, and then you say, "What would you have me do? What would be the most loving way for me to act at this point?" And then you do it. You first try to be aware of your own interference. Again, whether someone's sickness brings out a lot of pity in you, guilt, pain, or hurt, or whether someone's behavioral characteristics bring out a lot of anger in you—that is what you pray for help with. And then say, "What would be the most loving thing for me to do? What would you have me do?" Whatever words you want to use are fine, but you certainly do not deny what you see. This is not a course in denial. In fact, the text says, in a passage I read from earlier, that it is almost impossible to deny one's physical experience in this world. It is not suggesting that we do that, because the next line says that this is a particularly unworthy form of denial (text, p. 20; T-2. IV.3:8–11).

Principle 30

By recognizing spirit, miracles adjust the levels of perception and show them in proper alignment. This places spirit at the center, where it can communicate directly.

Principle 30 is the same as Principle 23. Basically, the miracle shows us that the problem is not in the body—it is in the mind. It is a problem of our guilt, and our guilt is a defense against the love that we really are. Therefore, the true center of our being is not the ego. It is not guilt; it is spirit. The Course teaches us that perception is an interpretation, not a fact. We see what we want to see or what we need to see—like hearing or seeing water in a desert. We cannot change the world, but we can change how we look at it. We replace the guilt of our egos, which we have made real, with the reality of our Identity as spirit, which the Holy Spirit is continually reminding us of.

Principle 31

Miracles should inspire gratitude, not awe. You should thank God for what you really are. The children of God are holy and the miracle honors their holiness, which can be hidden but never lost.

This is the same point I made earlier in referring to Jesus saying that we should not stand in awe of him. We should be grateful for the miracle because of the healing and peace that it brings, but we should not be in awe of it because it is something that exists here in this world. We should be in awe of the Source of the miracle, which is God, but not of the miracle itself.

This is another statement of the Atonement principle. The ego teaches that the holiness of Christ, the holiness of who we really are, has been lost because of our sin. Sin has changed the reality of Heaven; it has changed the reality of our relationship with God; it has turned us into miserable sinners and has turned God into a vengeful, avenging God. All that has become real. But all that has truly happened is that we have just fallen asleep and covered our holiness with veils of darkness. And now we believe that the dream is reality and that the reality is the dream. The truth about us, which is the fact that we are holy, can be hidden by our egos, but it has never been lost. The miracle shows us that the veil of evil is merely a defense against our holiness, a call for help and for love.

A Course in Miracles is amoral with respect to the whole question of evil or darkness in the world, and there being good things to do or bad things not to do. This is, of course, not the same thing as saying it is immoral. It does not have a morality because morality has to do with judging form or behavior. The Course's "morality" is the undoing of guilt. The Course is not "against" anything in the world; it is "against" guilt.

Q: What about feeling good when you get angry?

A: Of course you feel good when you get angry. In that instant when you are angry you believe that you have at last gotten rid of your guilt. And why should that not feel wonderful? It does, but only until the guilt rises up again in your awareness, now strengthened by the fact that you have attacked someone else unjustly.

Principle 32

I inspire all miracles, which are really intercessions. They intercede for your holiness and make your perceptions holy. By placing you beyond the physical laws they raise you into the sphere of celestial order. In this order you *are* perfect.

Obviously, Jesus is very clear that he is the source of the miracles, and it is a good thing, too. As *A Course in Miracles* says, we do not know our own best interests, let alone anyone else's, so that is why we should ask the one who does. If we try to act on our own, we are trying to be the inspirer of miracles, usurping the role of Jesus, just as we once did with God when we separated from Him.

The word "intercessions" here is deliberate. Jesus is not talking about intercessory prayer as it is usually thought of, or the idea that he intercedes between us and God which is the traditional view that God was too angry at us, so we needed someone who would be a go-between who could appease the wrath of God. He uses the word that has those connotations but, obviously, it is used differently. The way that he does intercede is between the holiness of Christ that we truly are and the self we believe we are, recalling to us the fact that we are holy and perfect and that everything else, whether we perceive something wrong in ourselves or in someone else, is merely part of the illusory system of the ego.

By our choosing a miracle, which means that we are choosing to hear God's Voice rather than the ego's, our perceptions become holy. Another word for holy perception, which is not usually used in the Course, is "true perception," a synonym for "the vision of Christ." It is the way that we perceive when there is no longer any guilt in us. We perceive through the eyes of the Holy Spirit when we no longer see someone as separate from us. This still occurs within the world of perception, which is this world. This does not mean that we deny someone else's body, but what we do deny is that the body has made us separate. We therefore deny all the perceptions and thoughts that would reinforce this separation of the ego.

"By placing you beyond the physical laws they raise you into the sphere of celestial order. In this order you *are* perfect." This is the same as the idea of how the miracle transcends the ego's laws, the physical laws. The culmination is that it restores to us the awareness of who we are, which is spirit. But this is not the goal of the Course, which is for us to be in this world without guilt.

Principle 33

Miracles honor you because you are lovable. They dispel illusions about yourself and perceive the light in you. They thus atone for your errors by freeing you from your nightmares. By releasing your mind from the imprisonment of your illusions, they restore your sanity.

This is another expression of the same idea. Miracles dispel all the illusions about our being separate, being bodies, about other people being bodies, and of our being victimized, either by ourselves or by other people. They help us recognize that we are all the same, that we are all in the same boat of the ego world together, and that we will leave this boat together. A phrase later on in the text says "together, or not at all" (text, p. 394; T-19.IV.D.12:8). Thus, no one left Heaven alone, and no one returns to Heaven alone.

"They thus atone for your errors by freeing you from your nightmares." We could read this as meaning that miracles correct our errors or undo our errors by showing us that there is another dream beyond the nightmare which corrects our illusions—and this is our "happy dream." "By releasing your mind from the imprisonment of your illusions, they restore your sanity." Our minds become freed from the illusory beliefs of the world.

Principle 34

Miracles restore the mind to its fullness. By atoning for lack they establish perfect protection. The spirit's strength leaves no room for intrusions.

This should be understood as meaning that miracles restore to the mind the awareness of its fullness, because the fullness or the abundance of God has never left. All that the miracle does is take away the veil that the ego had put there that kept hidden from us the abundance of who we really are. By atoning for lack (i.e., by correcting for lack), miracles establish protection. The ego teaches us that we are lacking something, which means we are vulnerable. This means that we have to be protected. What the miracle does is show us that there is no lack in us, and therefore we do not need any protection. The protection of spirit, thus, is merely the awareness of the invulnerability of spirit. A child of God can never be hurt. That is one of the clearest understandings we could have of the meaning of the crucifixion. That is what Jesus taught us: despite what the world perceived, nothing was being done to him. His body may have been attacked, but *he* could not have been attacked. He identified with the perfect protection of spirit because he knew Who he was and, therefore, it did not matter what was done to his body, whether physically or psychologically. That is the perfect protection of spirit. At that point, then, spirit cannot be intruded upon. It is as if there is a circle of light around us that we identify with, and any darkness that the ego would try to throw up to us would just be dispelled by the light. You cannot introduce darkness into a room full of light. Darkness is the absence of light, which really means that darkness has no properties of its own. Identifying with the light of Christ, Who we are, is our protection. What is interesting is that sometimes people try to concretize that in some way by trying to extend or manifest a circle of light around them, or they will beam light or something like that. All that does is make the body real and make danger real. Therefore, all you need to do is know Who you are, and that knowledge and that awareness is the light. You do not have to do anything. Once you do something, that becomes a defense. You do not *do* anything; you just remember Who you are, and that being is beyond all doing.

Principle 35

Miracles are expressions of love, but they may not always have observable effects.

This is very important. One of the traps that people fall into, as I have already said, whether they work with *A Course in Miracles* or they are into any other form of healing, is that they want results. If I do not get results, if your cold does not disappear, if the wound does not heal, if this tumor does not go away, then that means I am not a good healer. All that has happened is that we have fallen into the same trap of making the body real.

One of the major cautions the Course consistently expresses is: Do not make the error real. *A Course in Miracles* does not believe in sin; but if it did, the sin against the Course would be to make the error real. We make the error real by believing we have to do something for or against the error. Once we believe there is a problem on the level of the body which has to be healed, then we are making the error real. Trying to project a circle of light around you or around someone else is an example of making the error real, because then you are saying that the light must protect this person or myself against the darkness. Obviously, then, you are making the darkness real. You do not have to fight against something if it is unreal. You only fight against it or protect against it when you believe it is real. The protection the Course talks about is the protection of our thought system, which means that we correct the misthoughts that we have.

Q: That sounds kind of tough. My question is, can you have your cake and eat it too? For example, if you need aspirin, if you need to go for a little magic now and then...

A: I am not saying you should not do that. All I am saying is:

Do whatever it is that makes you feel better, but do not believe it is doing what you think it is doing. The Course talks about the idea of bringing illusions to the truth, or darkness to the light. The ego does it the other way around. It brings truth to the illusion. People will be tempted to take the truth of this Course, which is a very pure system, and bring it to the illusions that we all cherish. There are certain things we do not want to let go of, so if you are fond of circles of light, then you do not want to let that go. Or, if you are fond of asking for parking spaces, you do not want to let that go. And there is nothing here that says you have to let it go. Jesus is not up there with a whip. He is just saying that it is not going to give you what you want, that is all. If you want to indulge yourself along the way, I think that is fine as long as you recognize what you are doing. That is what is important.

A Course in Miracles does not say that we should not get angry. It says that we should not justify the anger. That is the mistake. Everyone is going to get angry, because we have egos. The idea is that when you do get angry and upset, do not justify it. That is what Jesus says in Chapter 3 when he talks about Atonement without sacrifice (text, p. 32; T-3.I). He says that that is where people went wrong. They had to reverse a whole way of thinking in order to justify the misperception that God caused His own Son to suffer. In other words, people created a theology that justified the projection of their own guilt. But when you construct a theology, psychology, philosophy, a theory of economics, or whatever to justify the projection of your own ego, you are going to have trouble. There is nothing wrong in having circles of light around you if that is what makes you feel better, but when you try to make them part of this thought system, that is where the mistake will enter in.

When you talk on Level One, everything does seem very hard, because that is the level which is uncompromising. It says you realize at the end that "what is false is false, and what is true has never changed" (workbook, p. 445; W-pII.10.1:1). Everything in this world is false and, therefore, you should not put any investment in it. But no one living in the world of the body, as we all are, is going to be able to totally let go of all investment in the world. There will always be some little

89

things, hopefully only little things, that we hold on to. That is Level Two, which is a much gentler way of looking at all of this. But what is uncompromising even there is the idea of not making the error real, not trying to justify the misperceptions of the ego. There is nothing wrong with having ego attacks; we are all going to have them. The mistake is in trying to say, "Well, this is what the Course is really saying," or "This is what the Bible is really saying," or "This is what God told me I should do." It is so much better to just say, "Well, I had an ego attack," or "It makes my ego feel better to have a circle of light around me," or to ask the Holy Spirit for a parking spot. That is fine as long as you do not try to say that is what this Course is saying. Once you do that, you will fall into the same trap as happened two thousand years ago, of taking a message that was radiantly pure and quickly putting shrouds of darkness and guilt all around it so that it ends up being a religion of hatred rather than one of love.

Q: I assume that indulging oneself, whether it is taking magic, taking naps, sexual pleasure, or any other kind of indulgence is okay, as long as you know that that is what you are doing. But, are we not then making the error real every single time we indulge ourself?

A: Yes, on Level One. But within our experience here in the world of the body (Level Two), such "indulging" can be a way of gently learning that this is not what I really want. But you do have to be careful that you are not deluding yourself, following the ego rather than the Holy Spirit, and thus getting involved in something that will hurt yourself and/or others, making your guilt even stronger. All that the Course would say is: Do whatever it is you want to do, but do not make it into the Kingdom of Heaven. Do not make a big deal out of it. That is the thing. What we usually do is make a big deal out of everything.

Q: But you are making the error real every time you do anything physical.

A: Of course! You cannot help that. But you make it worse when you try to justify it. It is much better to say that I still have this body and I believe I have certain needs, and there are certain things that give me pleasure; there are certain things I want to avoid because they give me pain. As long as I am a body, I am going to have those, but that does not mean anything. What is meaningful is that I forgive this person who works with me or who lives with me, and that I really want this relationship healed. The other stuff is kind of silly. The idea is to do whatever it is, but not to make a big deal of it. In fact, there is a line that comes near the end of this chapter that says that "physical impulses are misdirected miracle impulses" (text, p. 12; T-1.VII.1:3). That is another way of saying that making the body real, whether you are talking about sexuality, sickness, anger, or war, is a defense against who we really are. Specifically in terms of sexuality, it is referring to the idea that joining with people through the body will not make you feel peaceful or comfortable, because the only joining is through the mind.

In other words, we all yearn to be back home with God because that is the core of our problem. Somehow we feel that if we can get physically close to people, whether you are talking about sexually close or just physically close, somehow that will undo the separation. Obviously, it does not because the problem has nothing whatsoever to do with the body. Again, it is our use of the body that is the mistake, trying to justify or spiritualize something that has nothing to do with anything spiritual. Nothing of the body is spiritual. It is the use of it which is important.

Q: Could the Holy Spirit be saying to you that this is not the right thing to do because it reinforces a lack that you think is real? In other words, you need this pleasure at this time, so by falling into that pitfall of accepting it, you are reinforcing the lack.

A: Yes, if you are looking at this from a very practical point of view, I think the key thing is that if something becomes a preoccupation, such that I cannot be happy unless I sleep with this person, I cannot be happy unless I eat this certain food, I cannot be happy unless I get this certain car, and on and on, that that is a red flag. Then the attainment of this becomes the Kingdom of Heaven, and the absence of it becomes hell. When you get caught in that kind of a trap, it is a red flag that tells you you are dealing very strongly in special relationships, whatever the form. But the idea is not to make a big deal about something that is not a big deal. What *is* a big deal in this world is guilt, and the answer for that is forgiveness. That is what is important.

Q: Does the Course say anything about the resurrection of the body?

A: How could the body be resurrected if the body does not die? Just as the body cannot be healed because the body was never sick, the body cannot rise from the dead because the body never died. *A Course in Miracles* does talk a lot about the resurrection. Remember, the body does not do anything. It is the mind that does it. The resurrection is the awakening from the dream of death. What happened with Jesus is that he awoke from the nightmare world we are all in. In our perception of the world and certainly that of the people around him who did not understand what he was talking about, he rose from the dead. They could feel his presence. Therefore, they put two and two together and got five, which is something we are all good at doing. Jesus did appear to them in their minds, in the form in which they could accept him, which obviously would have to be in a form that they would identify as Jesus, which would be in the body. But his resurrection was really an awakening from this nightmare dream, which is a dream of death, of separation, murder, attack, assault, etc. But, again, the key to it is once you say the body resurrects, you are saying the body died, which means you are saying the body is real. The most powerful witness to the reality of the ego's world is death, because death says the body lived. If the body lived, then the ego must live and the entire ego thought system must be correct. What Jesus taught us is that the body does not die, the body does not rise, the body does not do anything and, thus, he remains with us despite what happened to his body. There is a line at the end of Chapter 15, written at Christmas time, which says: "The Prince of Peace was born to re-establish the condition of love by teaching that communication remains unbroken even if the body is destroyed, provided that you see not the body as the necessary means of communication" (text, p. 305; T-15.XI.7:2).

Q: Do you mean that he just took the form? How about when he appeared to the apostles?

A: He "appeared" in people's minds.

Q: And Thomas was told to touch his side?

A: I am not sure how much of that actually happened. John's gospel, especially, was written in part to combat what they thought was a threat from the Gnostics, who were already starting to be a real threat within Christianity. Some Gnostics taught that Jesus was not a body. These were called "docetists," a term derived from the Greek word meaning illusion. What that incident in the gospels shows, supposedly, is that Jesus had a body because Thomas touched him. I am reasonably sure that most scripture scholars would deny that that was actually an historical event. They would see it more in terms of the theology that John was teaching that Jesus was in a body; and that teaching was specifically aimed against the Gnostics.

Q: Are you discounting astral projections, then? This seems like a possible explanation of what some people thought they saw.

A: Am I discounting them? No, that is another way of looking at it; but it is still of the ego.

Q: Since he was described as going through walls, appearing and reappearing, it seemed...

A: You really have to question all the resurrection appearances in the gospels. Most scripture scholarship does do that. The resurrection appearances in the four gospels contradict each other. On basic facts they contradict each other, such as who saw him and when. The consensus opinion is that you are getting an expression of the emerging theology of the various Christian churches at the time rather than anything that is historical. That is why to try to say what Jesus did do or did not do is very difficult; no one really knows what he did in the first place. There is very little history in the gospels, but there is a lot of theology and people reading back into the story what they wanted to have there. By the way, the Course does not comment on that and does not deal with that.

Q: Saint Teresa would have interviews with Jesus in the palm of her hand. I understand her visions were very strongly perceptual.

A: Right. If you work with *A Course in Miracles* you must accept the premise that everything comes from our minds. There is nothing that is outside us. It is all a projection of what is within, which then means you can project anything you want. Psychologists have done this for years and years with projective tests. People see all kinds of things in perceptual stimuli that do not have specific recognizable forms, such as in the Rorschach ink blot test. We see what we want to see, which I do not think takes away from what the basic message of the gospel is at all. In fact, the Course really makes that message of forgiveness very, very clear.

We are still discussing Principle 35, that "miracles may not always have observable effects." What is important is the effect the miracle does have, which is to bring the miracle worker peace. In fact, when I turn my mind over to Jesus and I no longer see someone as attacking or being attacked, I will feel peaceful. What happens after that is between Jesus and the other person. I have done my part. The gift of my peace will be given to that other person, even though he or she may not accept it. This may mean that the miracle may not have observable effects. There is a series of three questions in the teacher's manual that deals with healing and makes this same point. One of the questions is, "Should healing be repeated?" (manual, p. 21; M-7). It has to do with a situation in which someone does not seem to be healed. The point is that if you believe someone has not been healed, you are making the body

94

real because you are looking for something on the level of the body.

Another area which has been hinted at here is covered in a lesson that says, "When I am healed, I am not healed alone" (workbook, p. 254; W-pI.137). Since all minds are joined and are one within this hologram, when my mind is healed and I extend peace, or peace is extended through me, it will touch all the other minds, most of whom I will not even be aware of. Since there is no reality to time as a linear expression, or to time at all, then this healing can occur through all dimensions of time. Obviously, we would have no awareness of this at all. Our only job, again, is to have our individual mind healed. What happens after that is up to the Holy Spirit.

Principle 36

Miracles are examples of right thinking, aligning your perceptions with truth as God created it.

A little later on, the Course uses the word "right-mindedness" (text, p. 21; T-2.V.3:1), i.e., thinking along with the Holy Spirit rather than the ego. The miracle does not directly express the truth of God, but it is aligned with it or reflects it. The truth of God is that we are all one. In this world, we experience the oneness by transcending all the ego barriers of separation: thoughts of anger, hurt, victimization, etc. While true perception is not the truth, it is nonetheless not in conflict with it. This is the same as the idea we discussed earlier about the "reflection of holiness," or the "heralds of eternity." These reflections are the goal of the Course, for they are the inevitable effect when we undo all the barriers to truth.

Principle 37

A miracle is a correction introduced into false thinking by me. It acts as a catalyst, breaking up erroneous perception and reorganizing it properly. This places you under the Atonement principle, where perception is healed. Until this has occurred, knowledge of the Divine Order is impossible.

"Erroneous perception" is perceiving a problem in the world, external to us. The miracle reorganizes perception because it shifts perception back to where the problem really is, in our minds. Jesus is the one who introduces the miracle. Our job is merely to choose to want him to, to ask his help to see the situation the way he does. This is true perception. Jesus takes the false perceptions we have made real—sickness, conflict, war, etc.—and turns them around so that we see everything the same way: everyone, including ourselves, is calling for help. The Atonement principle is then chosen, which can be restated as the denial of the reality of the separation and guilt.

Another technical term used consistently throughout *A Course in Miracles* is "knowledge." As the Course uses it, it is synonymous with Heaven. The counterpart to knowledge, or the opposite to knowledge, is perception, and almost always you will see those two terms juxtaposed. Knowledge transcends the subject-object dichotomy, which is inherent in perception. Even "holy visions" (such as those many mystics report) are perceptual and, therefore, do not last.

Knowledge is of spirit, of God, and cannot be attained in this world. In fact, the Course says very clearly that knowledge is not the goal of this Course; peace is (text, p. 128; T-8.I.1:1–2). Here it is talking about the peace that comes within this world when you look on all people as being joined with you. There is no guilt and no attack.

Principle 38

The Holy Spirit is the mechanism of miracles. He recognizes both God's creations and your illusions. He separates the true from the false by His ability to perceive totally rather than selectively.

This means that the Holy Spirit is a "switch-hitter" and, as the Course says later on, He is "the only part of the Trinity that has a symbolic function" (text, p. 67; T-5.I.4:1). This means He can function in a world of symbols. There are no symbols in Heaven, only in this world.

Q: If the separation is an illusion, and the Holy Spirit came into existence to solve that, is not the Holy Spirit an illusion?

A: No, because God created Him. It is a good question, though. The Course's answer is that when the separation is totally healed and the Holy Spirit is no longer needed, He still exists because God created Him. And then the Course says that He returns to Heaven and blesses our creations (text, p. 68; T-5. I.5:7).

Q: But it seems like He was created to solve a problem that does not exist.

A: That is right, and because he was created by God, which really means He is just an extension of God, once He does that, He cannot disappear. His *function* is an illusion, for it is to correct a problem which is inherently illusory, which means that this function, too, must be an illusion, as is the *form* in which the *content* of His Love is experienced by us.

Q: But He is one of us...

A: No, He is not one of us. We are part of the Second Person of the Trinity—Christ—and the Holy Spirit is the Third Person of the Trinity. On another level, of course, the Trinity is One. Nonetheless, *A Course in Miracles* does speak of Levels of the Trinity. This is more than a fine, theological distinction. It is important to correct the idea that the Holy Spirit's Voice is our own. This is similar to the belief that we are God, which the Course quite clearly states we are not. To believe that God's Voice is our own, let alone that we are God Himself, is just another expression of the basic separation belief that got us all in trouble in the first place.

Q: You used another kind of example. You said that God sent the Holy Spirit into the dream; He is not part of the dream, but He came into the dream to speak to us within it.

A: The question still is, "What happens when the dream is over?" It is one of those things no one could understand anyway. I can just tell you what *A Course in Miracles* says about it. But the idea is that the Holy Spirit has a foot in reality, in Heaven, and He has a foot in the dream (assuming He has two feet). He is within the dream, but yet He is not part of the dream. He is within our separated minds and works within them; yet He also is in touch with the Christ Mind. He is like an intermediary.

God, of course, does not even know about the dream, or the world of illusion. An analogy would be that of a parent looking in on a sleeping child at night and seeing the child thrashing around, obviously having a nightmare. The parent does not know what the child is dreaming, for it is outside his or her mind, but the parent does know that the child is in pain and would obviously like to alleviate that pain. That is the situation God is in. Therefore, He extends Himself into the dream, into the mind of His sleeping Son. The "Holy Spirit" is the name *A Course in Miracles* gives to this extension, the Voice for God. And within that dream He tells us, "My brother, choose again. You can look at your dream differently." Thus, He screens out what does not truly meet our need; i.e., special relationships. He helps us to unify our perception, to see all things as lessons God would have us learn. That is what is meant by "He separates the true from the false," and "to perceive totally rather than selectively." That was the point I was making earlier, that He would see all aspects of a situation. We would see a situation only in terms of our specific needs. He recognizes all situations as opportunities for healing all people who are involved.

Q: The aspect of the Holy Spirit that has one foot in one world, Heaven, and another foot in our world, the dream—does that mean that He can have both knowledge and perception at the same time?

A: Right.

Q: What does the Course mean by teaching that we are never in the wrong place at the wrong time?

A: We can never be in the wrong place at the wrong time because we can always learn from any and every thing. The Holy Spirit can use all situations and relationships to teach us the single lesson that the separation is unreal. On a deeper level, the statement reflects the idea that the script is already written. We have already been through all this. We are merely, as the Course says, reviewing mentally what has already gone by (workbook, p. 291; W-pI.158.4:5). And we can review or re-experience what has already happened either by choosing the ego or the Holy Spirit. Therefore, being in the right or wrong place has no meaning. The way that we review this place gives it its meaning.

Principle 39

The miracle dissolves error because the Holy Spirit identifies error as false or unreal. This is the same as saying that by perceiving light, darkness automatically disappears.

It is the same thing to say that He dissolves error, corrects errors, undoes errors, or atones for errors. He realizes that all errors are false or unreal. There are no gradations in errors. One times zero is the same as a hundred or a thousand times zero.

"This is the same as saying that by perceiving light, darkness automatically disappears." Once you perceive and recognize the truth of who you are, the errors or the darkness of the ego will disappear because all that holds them in place are your thoughts about them. Remember, there is nothing out there that is real. It is only our thoughts that make the things of the world real in our mind. And once we do make them real, the ego becomes real. And then we cannot overlook the ego. As the Course teaches, you cannot forgive a sin once you have made it real (e.g., text, pp. 593f; T-30.VI.1-3). We cannot say the world is illusory and nothing but a classroom in which we learn this as long as we believe that the darkness is real and needs healing and light. The light is not needed out there, because there is nothing out there. It is needed within our minds which believe in the darkness, and the darkness, of course, is nothing but our own guilt. This principle also reflects the idea that light and darkness are mutually exclusive states. When you turn on a light in a dark room, the darkness disappears. Turn the light off, and the darkness returns. That is how "sin" may be understood as well. Call something a sin, and it has become real and can no longer be seen as a call for help. Sins call for punishment; the call for help or love calls for help and love.

Principle 40

The miracle acknowledges everyone as your brother and mine. It is a way of perceiving the universal mark of God.

The error that the miracle corrects is the error of believing that we are separate. Whether we are separated by our bodies or separated by the terrible things we believe people do, all the miracle does is reflect the fact that we are one, and that is what Jesus is always reminding us of—that we are all one with him. The "universal mark of God" would be our sharing in the light of Christ.

Q: And it is sort of an inclusive system. No one is excluded.

A: No one is excluded. It could not be the Sonship if someone were excluded.

Principle 41

Wholeness is the perceptual content of miracles. They thus correct, or atone for, the faulty perception of lack.

Once again, we are saying the same thing. The basic principle of the ego is the scarcity principle, that there is something missing because we have excluded God. That is where guilt comes from: the thought that there is something lacking, which makes the ego and, therefore, the body real. We see other people and ourselves as lacking; the miracle reflects for us the wholeness that is our true Identity. "Wholeness" can be equated with abundance, the denial of the ego's scarcity principle. "Abundance" does not mean anything material, an association frequently made in what is called Prosperity Consciousness. In Prosperity Consciousness, it is typically thought that the abundance of spirit can be translated into material form: If I think abundance, then I will receive abundance. There is no question that our thoughts do influence what is outside us. This is how the whole physical world was made in the first place. But that does not make it into a spiritual principle. From the perspective of the Course, this is the mistake here. Our minds do affect the world, but this is merely a statement of the power of the mind. It is a psychic phenomenon, not a spiritual one. What makes it spiritual, as we have seen, is turning the power over to the Holy Spirit. Without His help and guidance we would merely continue to choose according to our ego's needs, rooting us still further in this world of illusion. Thus, the miracle does not give us material things. The miracle simply undoes the defenses that were based on our belief in lack and which reinforce this scarcity principle. This process then returns our mind to its original and ongoing state of being one with God, having everything that God gave us in creation: joy, unity, freedom, happiness, etc.

Again, please do not read the word "at-one" or "at-one-ment." At-one-ment is the state of our being in Heaven, where we are all at one with God and with each other. Atonement, however, has nothing to do with Heaven. It has to do with the state here, so if you want to use "at-one-ment," it would be in

101

the sense that atonement restores to us the awareness that we are at one with God.

Principle 42

A major contribution of miracles is their strength in releasing you from your false sense of isolation, deprivation and lack.

We feel that we are isolated from our true Self or from God, and we feel isolated from each other. Once we feel that we are separate, we will then project the blame for it onto other people and believe that they are depriving us. That is what deprivation comes from. Deprivation is the statement that says *you* are depriving me of something that I want, or need, or am. This projection is a denial of the fact that I had first taken it away from myself. Scarcity or lack must lead to deprivation, since guilt (another word for the belief in lack) must always be projected, a fundamental law of mind. It is the projection of the responsibility for having chosen to believe that we are lacking in something: I did not do this to me—you did. As the Course says, "The secret of salvation is but this: That you are doing this unto yourself" (text, p. 545; T-27.VIII.10:1).

Principle 43

Miracles arise from a miraculous state of mind, or a state of miracle-readiness.

Later on, this is called "right-mindedness" (e.g., text, p. 21; T-2.V.3:1). In other words, we first shift our mind from the ego, the wrong mind, to the Holy Spirit's way of thinking, which is the right mind. That is what the miracle is. We give up the investment in the ego's way of looking—attack, separation, etc.—and choose instead the Holy Spirit's—forgiveness and joining, seeing all things as opportunities to learn that we are forgiven.

Principle 44

The miracle is an expression of an inner awareness of Christ and the acceptance of His Atonement.

We can say that the miracle joins you with someone from whom you have separated. This reflects back to us the idea that we are all one in Christ, and this corrects the error of believing we were separated. Accepting Christ's Atonement is accepting this principle of being one with Him. Here again, we see the idea that the miracle is the expression of Christ, not the awareness itself. This is similar to what we talked about earlier—that the miracle is a reflection of the truth, not the truth itself. It still exists and has meaning only within the world of illusion.

Principle 45

A miracle is never lost. It may touch many people you have not even met, and produce undreamed of changes in situations of which you are not even aware.

This is similar to Principle 35. Think of the model of the hologram where we are all joined, and all the dimensions of time and space are in one part. There is no way that we could ever judge the power of what it means to let go of our grievances or to let go of our beliefs in separation. "When I am healed I am not healed alone" (workbook, p. 254; W-pI.137), as we have already seen. This can have effects, not only on people physically here, but on people who have already died. Time is not linear, and we are joined in one mind as in the hologram, regardless of the particular dimension of time and space we believe we or others are in.

Again, the only thing *A Course in Miracles* asks of us is to accept the Atonement for ourselves, which means to do our part in having our minds be healed of these thoughts. The extension of that miracle—Atonement or forgiveness—is not our concern, because we would have no idea of what is truly helpful. Our only responsibility—to accept the Atonement for ourselves—is to choose forgiveness or the miracle.

Q: What about intercessory prayer? How does that fit in?

A: It does not, at least not in the usual way of thinking about it. First, God does not have to be told what to do; it is simply insane to believe that. Second, and even more important, as I mentioned earlier, once we pray for others, we are saying there is a problem out there, and then we are right back in the ego's trap. We do not pray for others, we pray for ourselves—that our minds, which believed there was a form of darkness outside, be healed. The early sections of "The Song of Prayer" state this very clearly. We pray really for help to get ourselves out of the way, so that the Holy Spirit can extend through our mind to other minds.

Principle 46

The Holy Spirit is the highest communication medium. Miracles do not involve this type of communication, because they are *temporary* communication devices. When you return to your original form of communication with God by direct revelation, the need for miracles is over.

This reflects the idea that the Holy Spirit communicates from God to us. He is that bridge or Mediator between Heaven and hell, or reality and the dream. This, again, is a distinction between the miracle and revelation.

"When you return to your original form of communication with God by direct revelation, the need for miracles is over." When we are all finished with our homework, have completed our path, and have forgiven everyone who has to be forgiven, then we no longer need the Holy Spirit as a link to God because there is no longer any split mind that has to be linked back with God. Then we are restored to awareness of perfect oneness with Him. The goal of the miracle is not God but the shifting of perception that clears the way to God. That is the function of the Holy Spirit. The miracle only has meaning within the separated world.

Principle 47

The miracle is a learning device that lessens the need for time. It establishes an out-of-pattern time interval not under the usual laws of time. In this sense it is timeless.

Let me go over what I said earlier, and then we will apply it to this principle. The need we all share is to use time to help us realize there is no time, and to use time to get us off this carpet (see chart on p. 48). Let us say that we have a massive ego problem with certain specific people around certain specific issues, which would take a tremendously long period of time to get off this carpet.

The miracle lifts us above the world of time. Through our choosing to forgive this huge chunk of guilt, it carries us over and then drops us back down onto time. It establishes an "out-of-pattern time interval." Let us say, for example, that this time interval within the laws of the world would have been a thousand years. By lifting us above the world of time, carrying us over, and then dropping us back down, we saved that thousand years, and so that whole interval of time now has been abolished. Again, that is the idea of saving time. Let me repeat what I said earlier. A very difficult relationship—one that brings up a tremendous amount of anger, hurt, resentment, guilt, anxiety, etc.—then becomes a very powerful means, if we let it, for working through a huge chunk of guilt. For it is this deeply repressed guilt that has surfaced through the relationship. If you read the first paragraph on page 6 in the text (text, p. 6; T-1.II.6), you will see this process clearly discussed. It is a very nice encapsulated summary of much of what we have been talking about.

Helen once was complaining to Jesus: "How come my life is so difficult?" To anyone else, her life would not have seemed difficult. Externally, she did not have a very hard life, but internally it was very painful for her. She was complaining to him about it, and as an answer, he gave her the image of a mountain. Helen's understanding of the image and Jesus' explanation was: "You are walking through the mountain. It would be much easier, in terms of requiring less effort, if you walked up the mountain and then down the other side, but it would take you much, much longer. By walking through the mountain, which is much more difficult, you will save a lot of time. Walking through the mountain is walking through very difficult and very painful situations, which in the usual course of events would have taken you many, many lifetimes, which is the walking up the mountain and down the other side." *A Course in Miracles* aims at saving time by having more and more people have their minds healed more quickly so that the plan of the Atonement can be speeded up, so that people can find peace more quickly.

That is why for many people, when they begin working with the Course, things seem to get worse. It is not because God is punishing them. It is because the Holy Spirit has taken their request seriously. They are saying to the Holy Spirit, "I want to learn more quickly." That is why Goethe is reported to have said, "You always have to watch out for what you ask because you might get it." This is how the miracle works. In this sense, it is timeless because it undoes time. It still occurs within the dimension of time, but it abolishes time or collapses time.

The crucial point is understanding what the miracle does, and this cannot be emphasized enough—in fact, if you leave today with nothing else but this idea, you would have come away with a great deal—the miracle is the means that the Holy Spirit uses to teach us that we are not the victims of the world. Our problems are not what others or the world do to us, but rather what we believe we have done to ourselves. Let me repeat a line that I quote frequently: "Beware of the temptation to perceive yourself unfairly treated" (text, p. 523; T-26. X.4:1). I can be treated unfairly only by myself, and for that I have already been forgiven. This is the essence of the curriculum of *A Course in Miracles*.

Principle 48

The miracle is the only device at your immediate disposal for controlling time. Only revelation transcends it, having nothing to do with time at all.

Again, revelation unites us directly with God; the miracle, through undoing the beliefs of separation in our mind, joins us with each other. Revelation is not the correction—that is the miracle—but it helps us to remember that this is not the real world. The revelatory experience reinforces what is true and, thus, serves as a powerful reminder when we are tempted to believe in the reality of what is false.

Q: Does the Course think we can have the revelation while we are still bodies?

A: Yes, it says that revelation will be brief, fleeting, temporary. People will have experiences where they will feel a direct sense of God's Presence, where in that instant the entire world just disappears. *A Course in Miracles* would say that is possible but, again, it is not the goal and it is certainly not part of the theory at all. It really is not talked about at all after Chapter 1.

Principle 49

The miracle makes no distinction among degrees of misperception. It is a device for perception-correction, effective quite apart from either the degree or the direction of the error. This is its true indiscriminateness.

This is just a restatement of the first principle—"there is no order of difficulty in miracles." It is an elaboration of that same idea, that the miracle corrects the error, regardless of what it looks like, whether it seems to be a loving expression or a hateful expression, whether it seems to be a cosmic expression or just a purely individual expression. It does not make any difference, because errors are all the same. It is not the body that the miracle heals but our misperceptions of others, most especially our misperception that others are victimizing us. Rather, they are our brothers and sisters. If we accuse them of victimizing us, it is only because we have first accused ourselves of victimizing ourselves or others. As workbook lesson 134 says, whenever we are tempted to accuse anyone of anything, we should first stop and ask ourselves: "Would I accuse myself of doing this?" (workbook, p. 243; W-pI.134.9:3). This is one of the central themes of *A Course in Miracles*. It is one of those lines which summarizes the whole message of the Course. We are the victims only of our thoughts. This means that we can change them and not be imprisoned by others. Therefore, we have not victimized anyone, ultimately not even God, and this undoes the whole ego thought system.

This miracle principle is such a central part of the Course's teaching. Once we believe there are certain things in the world that are better than others or worse than others, we are falling into the trap. That would be the same trap, then, as talking about the resurrection of the body. This is a subtle way of making the body real and making the body the focus of attention. The body can be used by the Holy Spirit or by Jesus as a way of getting His message through. That is how the Course came through. But the idea is not that the body is real. It is just that it is serving a useful purpose.

A workbook lesson that is worth looking into is lesson 184, which talks about all the various names that the world has used as a substitute for the Name of God. All these names are symbols. But then the last half of the lesson explains that it would make no sense if we were asked to live in this world, take a teaching function, and yet go beyond all the names of the world. It explains how the Holy Spirit uses the symbols of this world to get His message through and how the basic pattern is to continue to go from the light we know as reality back into the darkness of this world, so that we bring a different message into the world—in other words, to be in the world and not of it. So, *A Course in Miracles* is not against using the symbols of this world—quite the opposite. It is just saying that they are symbols, and we should never lose sight of that fact nor the truth that is beyond the symbol. Recall the aforementioned section, "Beyond all Symbols" (text, p. 531; T-27.III). But remember, the Course does not say that you jump from one end of the carpet to the other, because that would just throw you into a panic. You go slowly, step by step.

Q: The text talks about everyone as experiencing at some time being out of the body. Do you think this refers to out-of-body experiences?

A: No, I do not think it does. It does not quite say it like that. It says an experience of being beyond the body (text, p. 361; T-18.VI.11). That could include out-of-body experiences, but what it is really talking about in that context is experiencing joining with something beyond the body, whether you are joining with a beautiful painting, a beautiful experience with a piece of music, or joining with a person if only for an instant, or identifying with some idea where you feel joined with something beyond the body. Now, that could include the out-of-body experiences some people have, but I do not think that it would be restricted to that.

Principle 50

The miracle compares what you have made with creation, accepting what is in accord with it as true, and rejecting what is out of accord as false.

Here is the distinction between "making" and "creating." The miracle compares what we have made, which is this world, with creation. This is similar to what is expressed in Principle 38. There are certain things that we do in this world that are in accord with creation, such as joining with people. It is not creation, but it is in accord with it because it follows the principle of oneness and of joining. Anything we do that unites us with each other from the Holy Spirit's point of view is truth. It is not truth on the level of Heaven, but it is truth because it reflects the truth of Heaven. If it is out of accord with that principle of unity, which means that we are separating ourselves from other people, then it is false. This is one way of recognizing or seeing the distinction between the two levels that I spoke about.

On Level One, truth is only of spirit, what God created. Falsity is everything else. On Level Two, truth is what the Holy Spirit can use to teach us what is true, and falsity is what will teach us that the ego is true. On Level Two, the truth is anything that is in accord with the Holy Spirit's will, which is anything that joins us with someone else. Falsity is something that would continue to separate us from someone else. If you see someone about to attack another person, on Level One, the whole thing you are seeing is an illusion. On Level Two, the illusion would be that this person is evil and sinful and is about to attack. That is the wrong-minded perception. On Level Two, what is true is that this person who seems to be attacking is really calling out for help. You do not deny what your eyes see; you just shift your interpretation. That is the crucial thing; you shift your interpretation. You see the seeming attack as a call for help. That is the vision Jesus had on the cross. He did not deny what people did. He denied what the ego would have said people were doing. He denied that people were evil, sinful, vicious, and were murdering him. Rather, he saw that they were calling out for the help and love they did not believe they deserved. That is the shift from the false perception of the ego to the true perception of the Holy Spirit, and that is what this principle is talking about.

Q: Could you say something about the holy instant?

A: The "holy instant," like many terms in the Course, is used in two different ways. One way would be a more individualized expression, which is that a holy instant is any instant in which we choose a miracle instead of a grievance, to join instead of separate. For example, there is someone that you are really furious at, and suddenly you are able to shift your perception and ask for help. That is a holy instant. It is defined as the interval of time in which the miracle is expressed. But then, there are other references where "the holy instant" is used for the end of time, such as that one big holy instant when the body is totally let go, when we reaffirm our identification with spirit and we are all home again. The word is used both ways, both in a much larger sense as well as in a more individual sense. And remember that choosing the holy instant only takes one, not necessarily both people in a relationship. It is always nice when both agree, but it is not necessary for healing to occur. Thus, while it takes two people to have a disagreement or argument, it only needs one to forgive. Both are forgiven for their belief in the reality of the separation when one remembers that he or she is not separate from the other.

Q: Does the Course say that once you experience a holy instant you will come back here and never feel the same? Am I just reading into this?

A: It teaches that once you have totally accepted the truth of this thought system, you will never look at this world the same way. The experience of most of us is that we do not totally accept it. We may accept it in one specific instance or a specific period of time, and then all of a sudden we go right back to the old way.

Q: But could you stay here?

A: If He asked you to. I am not sure that you would want to otherwise, but if you have done all your work, you have done what you came to do, and He asked you to stay for a while, well of course you would say yes, right?

Q: There is also a section in the manual that addresses that specifically: "Can God Be Reached Directly?" (manual, p. 61; M-26). It says that there are those who have reached God directly and then sustained that awareness in this world. Needless to say, these are few, but it is basically the same idea. It is possible, but it is very rare.

A: Yes; for most of us, we still have lots of work to do.

Q: Can you do this in one lifetime?

A: In principle, yes. Since the whole world and our experience here in the body is all a dream, then all that we need do is awaken from the dream and it is gone. That would be a Level

One perspective. However, on Level Two, in the world we believe we are in, the degree of fear that roots us here—the fear that God would destroy us if we ever relinquished our hiding place, which is the body—is so extreme, we require a gentler awakening process, as the Course frequently states (e.g., text, p. 542; T-27.VII.13:4-5). Within the illusory world of time, this process will take a long, long time, as *A Course in Miracles* also says at one point (text, p. 30; T-2.VIII.2:5). The Course says, as I mentioned before, that if we can forgive one person totally, we will have forgiven all of them. This is the same kind of statement. Our experience, however, is that we need to forgive many people, and the same person over and over. Our guilt, in effect, gets chipped away, rather than made to disappear in one huge chunk.

That is why it is important, if one works with the Course as his or her path, to have a healthy respect for the ego. A danger many people fall into is thinking that the ego can be done away with, one- two- three. All that really happens then is that people deny the ego rather than look at it and then change their minds about it. Thus, many choose to overlook the more difficult passages in the material that deal with special relationships and say instead that *A Course in Miracles* is about love, period. The Course is not about love; it is about guilt. By recognizing our guilt we are then able to let it go; then the Love of God is restored to our awareness. But we cannot skip over steps. This is one major advantage of being a psychologist: having this healthy respect for the ego, and understanding how deeply rooted we all are in its dynamics.

A Course in Miracles says, as we have seen, that when we come closer to the ego's foundation, when we begin listening to the Holy Spirit more than to the ego, the ego retaliates and becomes vicious (see above, p. 71). The Course means this literally. The ego's goal is murder, the Course says (text, p. 460; T-23.III.1:5), and it means this literally as well. To ignore these references is to miss the heart of the Course. And, it is also to miss the specific role of Jesus and the Holy Spirit in helping us through these painful periods of unsettling, as the Course in one place refers to this process (manual, p. 9; M-4. I.7:1). We need Their help in holding our hand, leading us through, when the ego's viciousness becomes so overwhelming. Then we can begin to experience the illusory nature of our guilt and fear, the "seeming terror" the Course refers to (text, p. 367; T-18.IX.3:7), and to know the Love of God that truly does uphold us.

Q: The body, the ego, the identification with the body as yourself—I am confused. Can you discuss that?

A: Essentially, *A Course in Miracles* talks a great deal, especially in the earlier chapters, about the ego-body equation. We are always equating ourselves with the body. One thing which is helpful to keep in mind is that the ego is more than the body. After the body dies, the ego is still around. Remember the ego is a thought system that is predicated on guilt. The body is merely the embodiment of the ego; the thought of the ego taking form, or the thought of separation taking form. The body is merely a learning instrument. It can either reinforce the teachings of the ego or it can reinforce the teachings of the Holy Spirit, which would ultimately teach us that we are not the body. We come into this world so we can learn certain lessons. We come into this world with a lot of excess baggage, our suitcases filled with all kinds of dirty clothes; our guilt, fears, etc. Whatever it is that we have not emptied out while we are here, whatever guilt we have not released or forgiven when our bodies die, we still take that with us. The name of the game, basically, is to get rid of as much of the dirty linen as possible—in other words, to let go of as much guilt as we can. Whatever we do not let go remains with us.

Once again, *A Course in Miracles* does not specifically treat the whole issue of past lives or reincarnation, but it certainly does imply it, and I think would therefore teach that whatever it is we do not forgive or let go of we take with us, and then we come back again. There is a very wonderful and moving passage which talks about the lifting of the final veil, the last obstacle to peace, which says: here you stand before this final veil, and you make the choice whether to pass through or wander off, only to come this way again (text, p. 393; T-19.IV.D.10:8). This is saying that you have the choice of really working this through now, or wandering off and coming back in whatever the form the lesson will take, to then learn that same lesson. Whatever it is that has not been healed, we take with us; the ego survives after the body dies. The ego is more than the body, and we just choose whenever we wish to—this is our choice—to come back into the world of the body so we can work through whatever parts of the hologram we have not worked through.

This is really a mind-boggling idea. Just because we believe we are in this particular dimension of time and space in New York State in 1985, does not mean that in another aspect of our mind we are not in ancient Greece or Palestine or some place 300 years from now. All that it means is that we are just tuning in to a certain part of the television set in our mind, and whatever it is we are tuning in to we are making real. What makes that seem so mind-boggling is the belief that time is linear. It is not linear. And certainly, some of the quantum physicists are teaching us the same thing. The linearity of time is just part of the same ego ploy to convince us that the guilt of the past is real and is projected into the future in terms of fear, and that that is what our reality is.

Q: I want to get back to the resurrection of the body. That is an article of faith in the Catholic Church. Is the Course saying that that particular article of faith is in error?

A: Yes, it is. Another article of faith in the Catholic Church states that God created the world, and that He created us in His own image and likeness. The Course would say all this is part of the same system. From the point of view of the Catholic Church, *A Course in Miracles* is in error. That is why I think one of the real benefits of the Course is that it is so clear that it is not the only path. It says at one point that "a universal theology is impossible" (manual, p. 73; C-in.2:5). It would have to be impossible because it is dealing with forms, symbols, and language, and no one shares all the same forms, symbols, and languages. It does say, however, that "a universal experience is not only possible but necessary" (manual, p. 73; C-in.2:5). To reach that universal experience the Holy Spirit must use different theologies, and theologies will conflict. But, if you are looking for trouble you will find it, and you will find conflict.

Q: I do have a conflict with the idea of God not being in the world. It has something to do with the influence of Teilhard de Chardin and how matter is spiritualized—we are all one, and we cannot separate body and spirit. I guess I am really finding a lot of meaning in that, and then the Course is saying something else.

A: I understand that. It is a different system. Many people, and Teilhard would certainly be among them, would say that you can unify mind, body, and spirit, that kind of holistic idea. That would not be the approach of the Course because the body does not exist outside of the mind. The Course really has a totally different conceptual system.

I gave a workshop recently, and someone brought up the example of Mother Teresa. She obviously seems to be guided by Jesus, who is guiding her in a way totally different from the way he has guided the Course. The question was, "How would I reconcile that?" I said that he gives people different messages in different forms that work for different people. I have had the good fortune of meeting her several times, and I do think she is guided by Jesus. I think that she is a very holy lady, within the context of what we mean by that, and I think hers is a totally different path from the Course: one of suffering, sacrifice, and following the teachings and doctrines of the traditional Roman Catholic Church. But the world needs her and what she is doing, just as it needs the Course.

Q: The plan of Atonement is for all paths?

A: Yes, *A Course in Miracles* is part of the plan of the Atonement. It is not *the* plan of the Atonement.

Foundation for "A Course in Miracles"
Conference and Retreat Center

Kenneth Wapnick received his Ph.D. in Clinical Psychology in 1968 from Adelphi University. He has been involved with A COURSE IN MIRACLES since 1973, writing, teaching, and integrating its principles with his practice of psychotherapy. In 1982, with his wife Gloria, he began the Foundation for "A Course in Miracles," and in 1988 they opened a Conference and Retreat Center in upstate New York. The following is their vision of the Foundation and description of the Center.

In our early years of studying *A Course in Miracles*, and of teaching and applying its principles in our respective professions of psychotherapy, teaching and school administration, it seemed evident that this was not the simplest of thought systems to understand. This was so not only with respect to the intellectual grasp of its principles, but perhaps even more important, in the application of these principles to one's personal life. Thus, it appeared to us from the beginning that the Course lent itself to teaching, paralleling the teaching of the Holy Spirit in the daily opportunities within our relationships that the manual discusses in its early pages.

One day several years ago while Helen Schucman and I (Kenneth) were discussing these ideas, she shared a vision that she had of this Center as a white temple with a gold cross atop it. Although it is clear that this image was symbolic, we understood it to be representative of what the Conference and Retreat Center was to be: a place where the person of Jesus and his message in the Course would be manifest. We have sometimes seen an image of a lighthouse shining its light into the sea, calling to it those passers-by who sought it. For us, this light is the Course's teaching of forgiveness, which we would hope to share and learn with those who are drawn to the Center's form of teaching.

We have always believed, moreover, that there was not to be *one* form or place of teaching, as this would be antithetical to the Course's principles. As the Course says in another context: "Are other teachers possible, to lead the way to those who speak in different tongues and appeal to different symbols?

Certainly there are" (manual, p. 56; M-23.7:2–3). The Center thus reflects our personal vision of *A Course in Miracles*. This vision entails the belief that Jesus gave the Course at this particular time in this particular form for several reasons. These include:

1) the necessity of healing the mind of its belief that attack is salvation; this is accomplished through forgiveness, the undoing of our belief in the reality of separation and guilt.

2) emphasizing the importance of Jesus and/or the Holy Spirit as our loving and gentle Teacher, and developing a relationship with this Teacher.

3) correcting the errors of Christianity, particularly where it has emphasized suffering, sacrifice, separation, and sacrament as inherent to God's plan of salvation.

In light of these statements, therefore, we view the Center's principal purpose as being to help students of the Course deepen their understanding of its thought system, conceptually and experientially, so that they may be more effective instruments of the Holy Spirit's teaching in their own lives. Since teaching forgiveness without experiencing it is empty, one of the Center's specific goals is to help facilitate the process whereby people may be better able to know that their own sins are forgiven and that they are truly loved by God. Thus is the Holy Spirit able to extend His love through them to others.

To help achieve these goals, we offer workshops and seminars on various topics, ranging from a general overview of the Course's thought system to concentrated studies of specific sections or themes. In addition, we welcome students who wish to stay at the Center for a period of time for private study and retreats.

The Center is situated on ninety-five acres in the Catskill Mountains, about 120 miles from New York City. Its country location and comfortable accommodations provide a peaceful setting in which students may carry out their plans for meditation, study, and reflection.

RELATED MATERIAL ON *A COURSE IN MIRACLES*

By Kenneth Wapnick

Books and Pamphlets

ABSENCE FROM FELICITY: The Story of Helen Schucman and Her Scribing of *A Course in Miracles.* The book focuses on Helen's lifetime conflict between her spiritual nature and her ego, and includes some of Helen's own recollections, dreams, letters, and personal messages from Jesus—all never before in print. Her own experiences of Jesus, relationship with William Thetford, and the scribing of the Course are highlighted.
ISBN 0-933291-08-6 • Paperback • 521 pages $16.

A VAST ILLUSION: Time According to *A Course in Miracles.* This book weaves together various passages from the Course to present a coherent statement of time, including its metaphysical nature, the role of the miracle and forgiveness in collapsing time, and finally the end of time. (This is an edited and expanded transcription of the tape album "Time According to *A Course in Miracles.*")
ISBN 0-933291-09-4 • Paperback • 301 pages $12.

LOVE DOES NOT CONDEMN: The World, the Flesh, and the Devil According to Platonism, Christianity, Gnosticism, and *A Course in Miracles.* An in-depth exploration of the non-dualistic metaphysics of *A Course in Miracles,* and its integration with living in this illusory world.
ISBN 0-933291-07-8 • Hardcover • 614 pages $25.

FORGIVENESS AND JESUS: The Meeting Place of *A Course in Miracles* and Christianity. Fourth Edition. This book discusses the teachings of Christianity in the light of the principles of the Course, highlighting the similarities and differences, as well as discussing the application of these principles to important areas in our lives such as injustice, anger, sickness, sexuality, and money.
ISBN 0-933291-01-9 • Paperback • 355 pages $16.

THE OBSTACLES TO PEACE. Edited transcript of tape album; line-by-line analysis of "The Obstacles to Peace" and related passages.
ISBN 0-933291-05-1 • Paperback • 296 pages $12.

A TALK GIVEN ON *A COURSE IN MIRACLES*: An Introduction. Fourth edition. Edited transcript of a workshop summarizing the principles of the Course; includes the story of how the Course was written.
ISBN 0-933291-16-7 • Paperback • 138 pages $4.

UN CURSO EN MILAGROS: UNA INTRODUCCION BASICA. This is the Spanish translation of A TALK GIVEN ON *A COURSE IN MIRACLES*: An Introduction. This Spanish edition includes a glossary of some of the more important terms used in the Course.
ISBN 0-933291-10-8 • Paperback • 152 pages $4.

BETRACHTUNGEN ÜBER *EIN KURS IN WUNDERN*. This is the German translation of A TALK GIVEN ON *A COURSE IN MIRACLES*: An Introduction. This German edition includes a glossary of some of the more important terms used in the Course.
ISBN 0-933291-12-4 • Paperback • 164 pages   US $8 DM 14

GLOSSARY-INDEX FOR *A COURSE IN MIRACLES*. Third edition. Summary of the Course's theory; more than 125 terms defined and indexed; index of over 800 scriptural references; line-gauge included to assist use of index.
ISBN 0-933291-03-5 • Hardcover • 308 pages $16.

CHRISTIAN PSYCHOLOGY IN *A COURSE IN MIRACLES*. Second edition. Discussion of the basic principles of the Course in the context of some of the traditional teachings of Christianity.
ISBN 0-933291-14-0 • Paperback • 90 pages $4.

Audio tape of the first edition, recorded by Kenneth Wapnick. $5.

OVEREATING: A Dialogue. An Application of the Principles of *A Course in Miracles*. This pamphlet presents the Course's approach to issues such as food addictions and pre-occupation with weight. (An edited and slightly expanded version of the tape, "Overeating.")
ISBN 0-933291-11-6 • Pamphlet • 35 pages $3.

AWAKEN FROM THE DREAM. Gloria and Kenneth Wapnick. Presentation of the Course's principles from a new perspective. Includes background material on how the Course was written.
ISBN 0-933291-04-3 • Paperback • 135 pages $10.

Video Tape Albums

SEEK NOT TO CHANGE THE COURSE. Reflections on *A Course in Miracles*. Talk given by Gloria and Kenneth Wapnick, including questions and answers, on some of the more common misunderstandings about the Course.
135 mins.   VHS $30. Audio tape version $15.

FOUNDATION FOR "A COURSE IN MIRACLES" Conference and Retreat Center. Gloria and Kenneth Wapnick speak about the Course's beginnings, the origin and purpose of the Foundation, and their vision of its development in the future. A visual and verbal portrait of the Center.
24 mins.   VHS $10.

Audio Cassette Albums

RECORDED SEMINARS AND WORKSHOPS

THE SIMPLICITY OF SALVATION. Intensive overview of the Course. 8 tapes $65.

HOLY IS HEALING. Psychotherapeutic applications of the Course. 8 tapes $65.

ATONEMENT WITHOUT SACRIFICE. Christianity, the Bible, and the Course. 2 tapes $15.

THE END OF INJUSTICE. Overview of the Course. 6 tapes $45.

THE EGO AND FORGIVENESS. Introductory overview of the Course. (Album consists of first two tapes of "The End of Injustice.") 2 tapes $15.

THE GIFTS OF GOD. A discussion of the inspired poetry of Helen Schucman, scribe of the Course; includes personal reminiscences about Helen. 3 tapes $24.

THE ORIGIN OF *A COURSE IN MIRACLES*. The story of the scribing of *A Course in Miracles*; reflections on Helen Schucman and William Thetford. 1 tape $6.

I WILL BE STILL AN INSTANT AND GO HOME. A collection of two talks and a meditation by Kenneth Wapnick, and one talk by Gloria and Kenneth Wapnick—given at various Sunday services. 1 tape $6.

LOVE DOES NOT OPPOSE. The importance of non-opposition as the basis of forgiveness in special relationships. 8 tapes $65.

JESUS AND THE MESSAGE OF EASTER. The Course's view of Jesus, and the meaning of his crucifixion and resurrection. 8 tapes $65.

THE AUTHORITY PROBLEM. The authority problem with God and its reflection in our everyday life. 5 tapes $40.

OUR GRATITUDE TO GOD. Our gratitude to God, to Jesus, and to each other; the obstacles and resistances to this gratitude. 5 tapes $40.

SICKNESS AND HEALING. Discussion of the cause and purpose of sickness in the ego thought system; analysis of healing as occurring in the mind—the healing of the belief in guilt, by turning to the Holy Spirit and forgiving. 8 tapes $60.

WHAT IT MEANS TO BE A TEACHER OF GOD. Discussion of the ten characteristics of a teacher of God, magic, and healing. 6 tapes $48.

OVEREATING: A DIALOGUE BASED UPON *A COURSE IN MIRACLES*. The ego dynamics involved in food addictions and weight problems; forgiveness through the Holy Spirit as the solution. 1 tape $6.

TO JUDGE OR NOT TO JUDGE. The Course's teachings on judgment; the process of recognizing our need to judge, and letting Jesus or the Holy Spirit judge for us. 4 tapes $32.

HEALING THE UNHEALED HEALER. The characteristics of the unhealed healer; healing through joining with Jesus in understanding all forms of sickness and problems as calls for love. 8 tapes $65.

THE REAL WORLD: OUR HOME AWAY FROM HOME. A discussion of our true home in Heaven, the ego's home in the world, and the Holy Spirit's correction of the ego's world: the real world. 8 tapes $65.

TRUE EMPATHY: THE GREATER JOINING. The world's version of empathy contrasted with the Holy Spirit's true empathy. 8 tapes $65.

JESUS: THE MANIFESTATION OF THE HOLY SPIRIT. A discussion of Jesus and the Holy Spirit in the context of the difference between appearance and reality, and the importance of Jesus as our guide leading us out of the dream. Included also is a discussion of the relationship of Jesus to Helen Schucman and to *A Course in Miracles*. 5 tapes $40.

THE LAWS OF CHAOS: OUR WAR WITH GOD. An in-depth exploration and discussion of the five laws of chaos that form the foundation of the ego's thought system, and powerfully express the ego's defenses against the love of God. 12 tapes $85.

"THERE MUST BE ANOTHER WAY." The words that led to the birth of *A Course in Miracles* provide the theme of this workshop which discusses forgiveness as the "other way"—rather than specialness—of relating to ourselves, each other, and to God. 1 tape $6.

THE METAPHYSICS OF SEPARATION AND FORGIVENESS. A summary of the teachings of *A Course in Miracles*, specifically showing how the principle that the thought of separation and the physical world are illusions becomes the foundation for the understanding and practice of forgiveness in our daily lives. 1 tape $6.

THE WORKBOOK OF *A COURSE IN MIRACLES*: ITS PLACE IN THE CURRICULUM • THEORY AND PRACTICE. A discussion of the metaphysical principles underlying the lessons, the mind-training aspects of the workbook, Jesus' gentle teaching method, and students' common misuses of the workbook. Two charts and an annotated outline of the workbook included. 8 tapes $65.

LINE-BY-LINE ANALYSIS OF KEY SECTIONS IN THE COURSE

THE FIFTY MIRACLE PRINCIPLES OF *A COURSE IN MIRACLES* 3 tapes $24.

THE WORLD ACCORDING TO *A COURSE IN MIRACLES* - 3 tapes $24.

THE OBSTACLES TO PEACE - 6 tapes $48.

SPECIAL RELATIONSHIPS—PART 1 - 8 tapes $65.

SPECIAL RELATIONSHIPS—PART 2 - 6 tapes $48.

TIME ACCORDING TO *A COURSE IN MIRACLES* - 6 tapes $48.

JESUS AND *A COURSE IN MIRACLES* - 5 tapes $40.

CAUSE AND EFFECT - 8 tapes $65.

PSYCHOTHERAPY: PURPOSE, PROCESS AND PRACTICE - 7 tapes $56.

THE SONG OF PRAYER - 10 tapes $80.

Please see the next page for ordering information.

Ordering Information

Prices include shipping (Book Rate) on U.S. orders. For quicker delivery (UPS), please call the Foundation. For orders shipped *outside* the U.S. only, please add the following for surface mail: for books and tape sets, $3.00 for the first item, $1.00 each additional item (pamphlets $.75).

New York State residents please add local sales tax. VISA and MasterCard accepted.

Order from:

Foundation for "A Course in Miracles"
R.R. 2, Box 71
Roscoe, NY 12776-9506
(607) 498-4116 • FAX (607) 498-5325

* * * * *

A COURSE IN MIRACLES and other scribed material
may be ordered from:

Foundation for Inner Peace
Box 1104
Glen Ellen, CA 95442
(707) 939-0200

A COURSE IN MIRACLES:
        Hardcover: $40
        Hardcover–combined volume: $30
        Softcover–combined volume: $25

PSYCHOTHERAPY: PURPOSE, PROCESS AND PRACTICE: $3.00

THE SONG OF PRAYER: PRAYER, FORGIVENESS, HEALING: $3.00

THE GIFTS OF GOD: $21.00

Additional copies of this book may be obtained by sending a check or money order for $8.00 per copy (includes fourth class postage) to:

Foundation for "A Course in Miracles"
R.R. 2, Box 71
Roscoe, NY 12776–9506
(607) 498–4116 • FAX (607) 498-5325